Modern Jewelry—Design and Technique

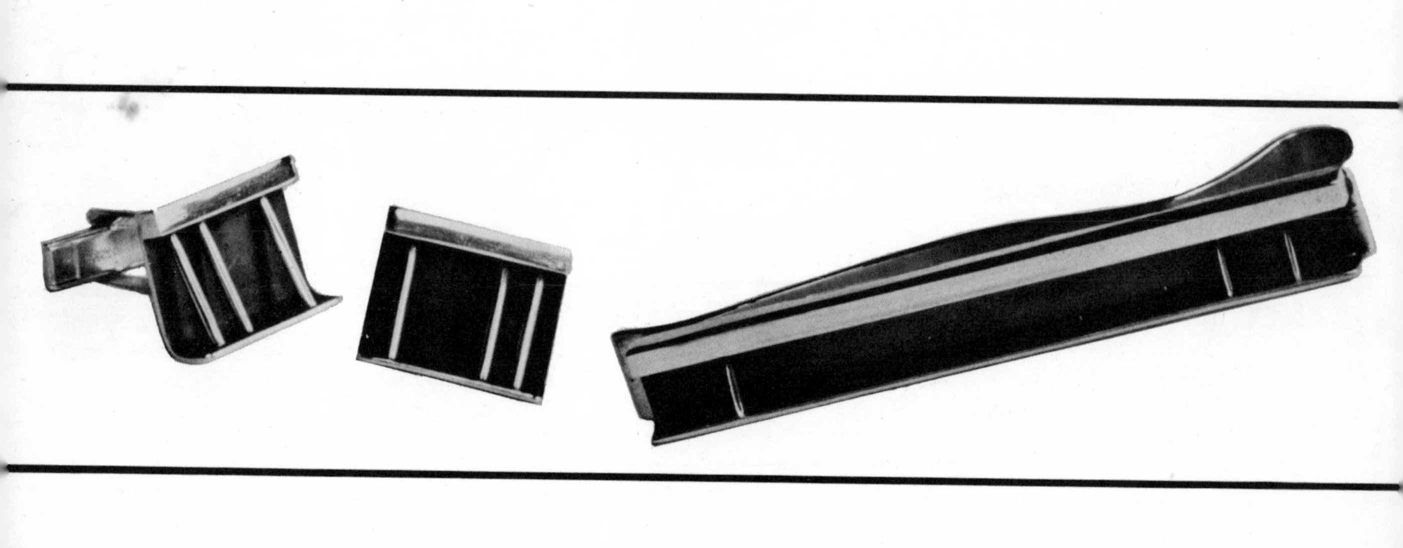

Irena Brynner

Modern Jewelry—Design and Technique

Reinhold Book Corporation
A subsidiary of Chapman-Reinhold, Inc.
New York Amsterdam London

I dedicate this book to my mother, who has worked by my side for many years and who is always a great inspiration to me; and to my students and all young artists.

Frontispiece

Constructed silver cuff links and tie bar with oxidized center panels. (Tatsuo Ishimoto.)

All casting was done by Billanti Casting Company, New York.

Printed in the United States of America
Library of Congress Catalog Card Number 68-16023
Designed by Emilio Squeglio
Type set by Graphic Arts Typographers, Inc.
Printed by New York Lithographing Corp.
Bound by Montauk Book Manufacturing Company, Inc.
Published by Reinhold Book Corporation
A subsidiary of Chapman-Reinhold, Inc.
430 Park Avenue, New York, N.Y. 10022

Contents

Introduction 6
Equipment and Techniques 42
Constructed Jewelry 42
Forged Jewelry 49
Wax-Modeling 54
Working with Sheet Wax 54
Texturing 65
Building a Ring 70
Working with Wax Wires 80
Sculpture 84
Bibliography 94
Suppliers 95

INTRODUCTION

I teach creative jewelry-making at the Art Center of the Institute of Modern Art affiliated with The Museum of Modern Art in New York City. Students from my Museum classes and young artists who come to visit me in my shop often ask me why I am doing this kind of work and how I got started. I am willing and happy to share my experiences with others and will try briefly and sincerely to tell about it in these pages. I teach on the basis of my experiences and hope that sharing them with others will give some help to those who start on a similar path.

In 1949 I did not know a thing about jewelry. I had received my art education—both academic and practical—at the university and art school in Lausanne, Switzerland, and later took private lessons in sculpture and painting. The Impressionist painters were my favorites, and I was barely acquainted with art movements after that period. I lived in northern China all through the Second World War and came to the United States in 1946. At that time sculpture was my life's aim.

I settled in San Francisco and, during my first two years there, worked ten to twelve hours a day in the studio of the sculptor Michael Von Mayer—a man who gave me a wonderful grounding in the technique of clay-modeling. I worked mainly with the human head and figure, one of the best sources for acquiring a knowledge of form—beautiful, subtle, flowing form. I particularly loved portrait work in sculpture and painting and concentrated my efforts in this area. Until 1948 no fresh breeze of contemporary art touched me; then I met the California sculptor Ralph Stackpole with whom I worked on stone sculpture, and who introduced me to the works of Miró, Picasso, and contemporary American artists. He took me to museums where like a child I began to see the world through new eyes. It was a revelation to me. I liked things which previously I would not even look at. As a result, I started to work in a way that would loosen up my style. I went to "life" classes where the model did not hold a set pose, but instead moved constantly but slowly, making it imperative to sketch as fast as possible. Sometimes I was only able to indicate the movement with a few quick strokes. This kind of freedom of expression sparked my imagination and filled my life with new excitement. Very timidly I began to introduce abstract forms into my work, but it was forced, and I did not feel sincere about it.

During this same period I saw my first piece of contemporary jewelry—a necklace by Clair Falkenstein. It enchanted me. Gradually I became more and more interested in crafts, especially in those crafts which were related in technique and form to sculpture.

At this time I knew I would have to choose a new creative medium. I could not make a living at sculpture without having to accept portrait commissions, and I did not want that restriction. I wanted to be free to express myself with sincerity, and a craft seemed to offer this. I had tried pottery, but felt it was too narrow since, in the end, the form always had to be a vessel or container. Jewelry seemed less limiting, and after serious consideration, I chose it.

Clair Falkenstein's necklace was a contributing factor in this decision.

I got a job as an apprentice with a jeweler in San Francisco and worked with her for about two months in the autumn of 1949. Then, before Christmas of the same year, Franz Bergman, a painter, ceramicist, and jeweler, hired me to make up his jewelry designs while he worked on ceramics. I will always be thankful for that experience. I was responsible for the work from start to finish. The process was shown to me step by step on the first piece, then I was left to do the rest. I have wonderful memories of those days—days so full of new discoveries and experiences. It was only a pre-Christmas job which lasted three or four weeks, but however short this span of time, it gave me a very good start.

After my job was finished, Mr. Bergman told me that he thought I had a talent for jewelry-making and advised me to continue it on my own. So in January, 1950, I went to adult education classes. I learned how to work out my ideas and where to get all the

(text continued on page 14)

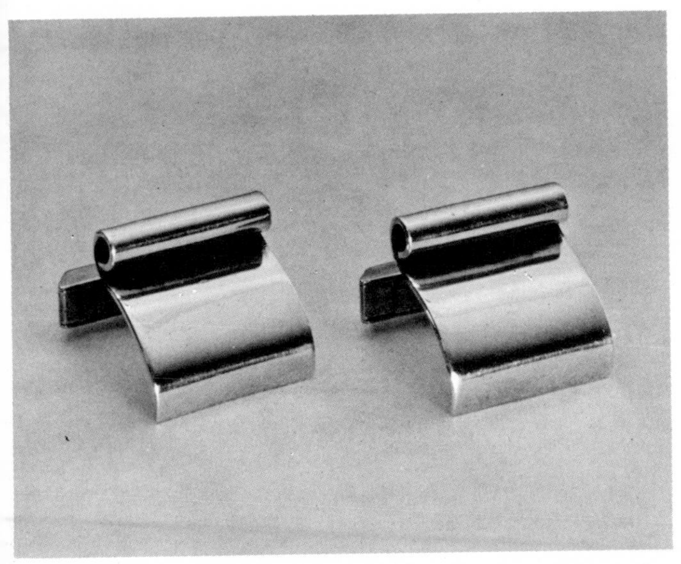

Constructed silver cuff links. (Tatsuo Ishimoto.)

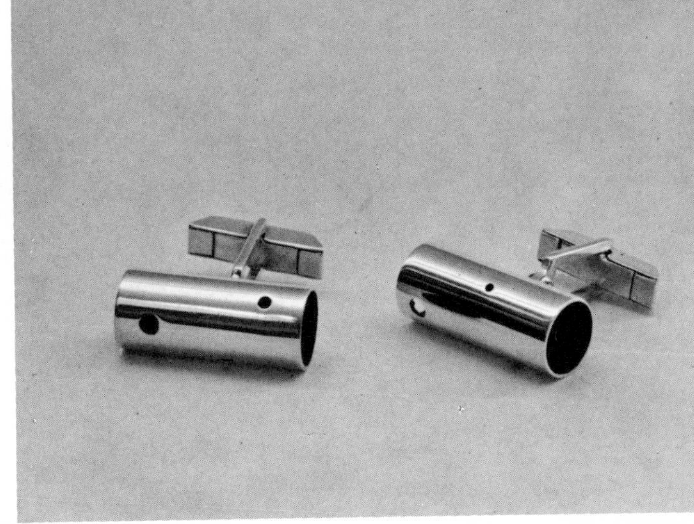

Constructed silver cuff links. (Tatsuo Ishimoto.)

Constructed and forged gold ring set with jade. (Tom Yee.)

Constructed gold ring set with jade. (Tom Yee.)

Right. Gold cast sculpture on amethyst crystals. Length 3½ inches. (Tom Yee.)

Below. Forged gold necklace and earrings with ancient Egyptian beads. (Tom Yee.)

Forged gold necklace and earrings set with gem oriental jade. (Tom Yee.)

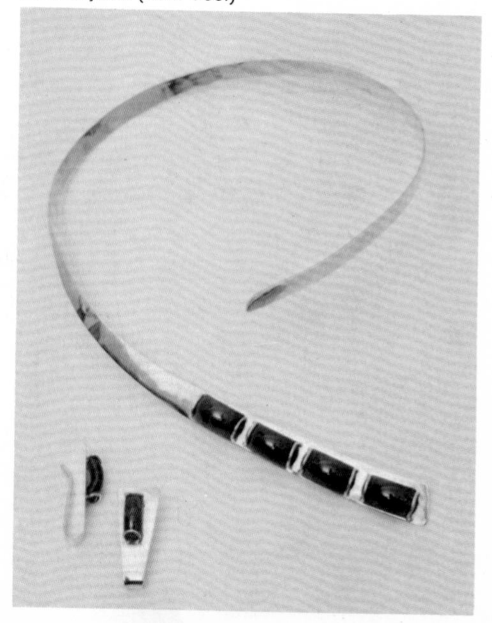

Opposite Page
Above left. Cast gold ring with free-set pearl. (George Straus.)

Above right. Forged and cast gold necklace set with amber. (Tom Yee.)

Below left. Forged gold necklace with rutilated quartz and Chatham emerald. (Tom Yee.)

Below right. Constructed white and yellow gold ring set with 64-kt. tourmaline and black pearl. (Tom Yee.)

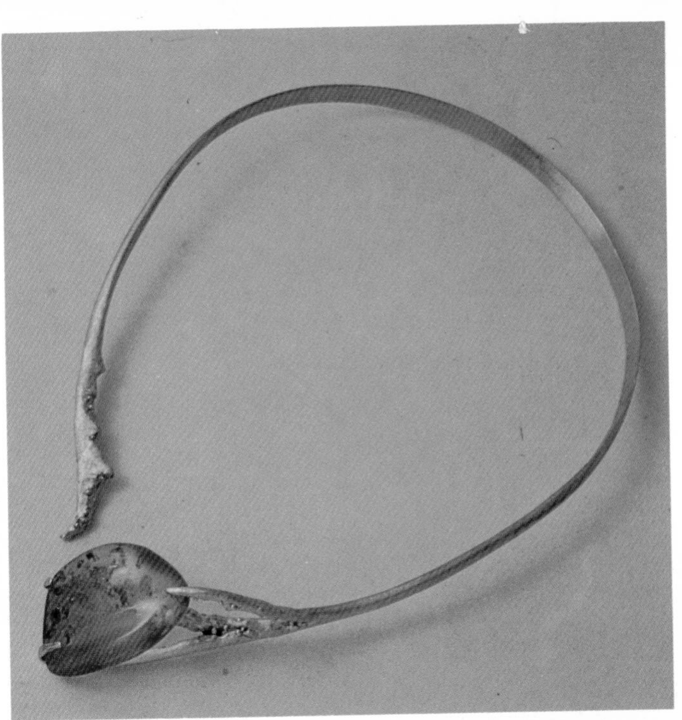

Right. Constructed gold ring set with a canary diamond. (Tom Yee.)

Below. Constructed yellow and white gold interlocking wedding and engagement rings with black jade stone. Lapidary by F. J. Sperisen. (Tom Yee.)

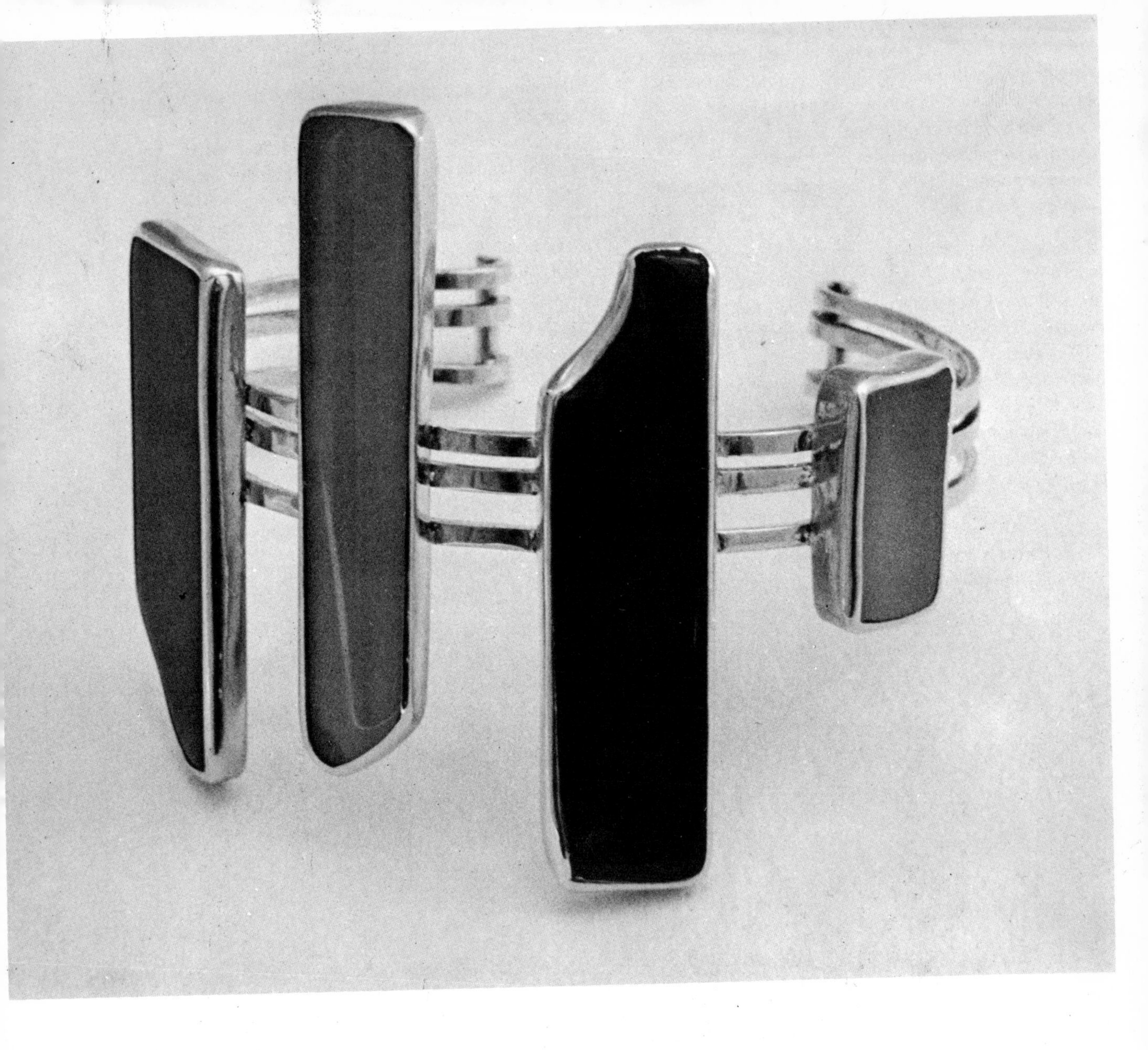

Constructed gold bracelet set with agates. (George Straus.)

necessary equipment to start working at home. The first year or year and a half, my equipment was very primitive—a washing machine motor served as a polisher; a Bunsen burner and small alcohol torch were my sources of heat. I had files and pliers and did my soldering on a metal ironing board. It was simple, but I think it is very good to get along with the minimum.

In March of the same year, with one pin and pair of cuff links, I went to Casper's, a furniture store with a small jewelry section, and one of the nicest shops in town. Bob Hight, the manager, looked at my work. The pin was really quite horrible, but the cuff links were good. He was interested in buying them and wondered if I had more. I did not, but did not say so, saying instead that I would return with more in a week. Shortly afterwards, Nany's, a San Francisco store specializing in contemporary jewelry, started buying my work. I was becoming a jeweler.

My early pieces were all constructed work made of wire and sheet silver which was cut into different shapes, fitted, filed, and soldered together. From the very start my work was three-dimensional, reflecting my training in sculpture, and I felt free and sincere in making abstract forms in jewelry as I had not in sculpture. The forms in jewelry had a decorative purpose. I did not have to create a mood or convey ideas. However, it was always something real—a concrete form—that gave me my ideas. For instance, for my very first piece of jewelry, the pair of cuff links I sold at Casper's, I imagined an unrolled scroll suspended from a horizontal bar with strings or wires attached to the bar, holding the edge of the scroll open (see title page).

After my first group of cuff links, I got interested in earrings. Most of my earrings derived from mobiles. Without really knowing it then, I had started working on abstract sculpture—only it was sculpture suspended from the ear. The forms were straightforward, simple in technique, but graceful.

At about that time (1950) I started to participate in open-air art shows in San Francisco, and much of

(text continued on page 22)

Constructed silver wire earrings. (Tatsuo Ishimoto.)

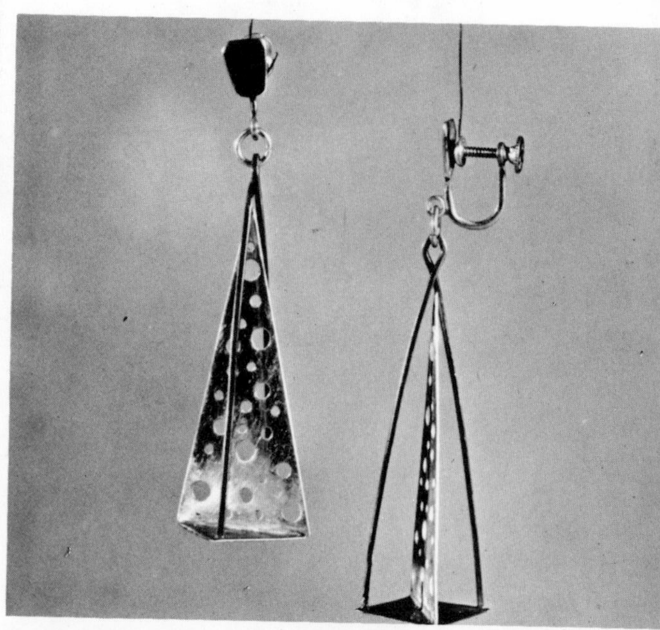

Constructed silver earrings. (Tatsuo Ishimoto.)

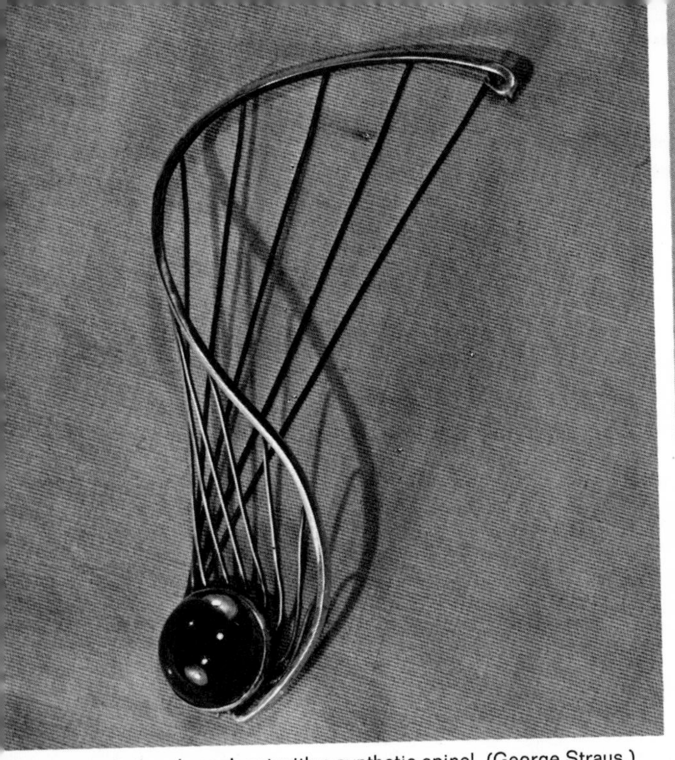

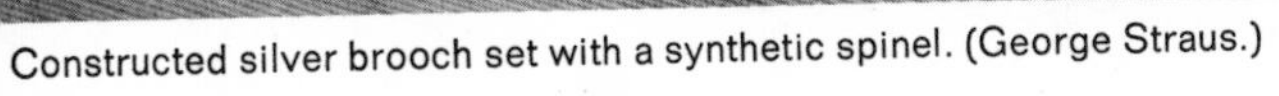

Constructed silver brooch set with a synthetic spinel. (George Straus.)

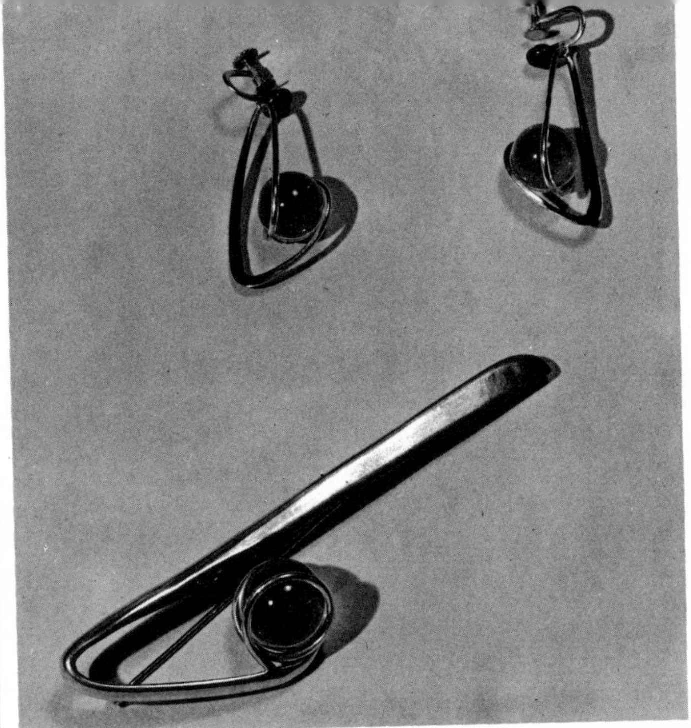

Constructed and forged silver earrings and pendant set with rock crystal.

Constructed silver ring with two pearls. (Tom Yee.)

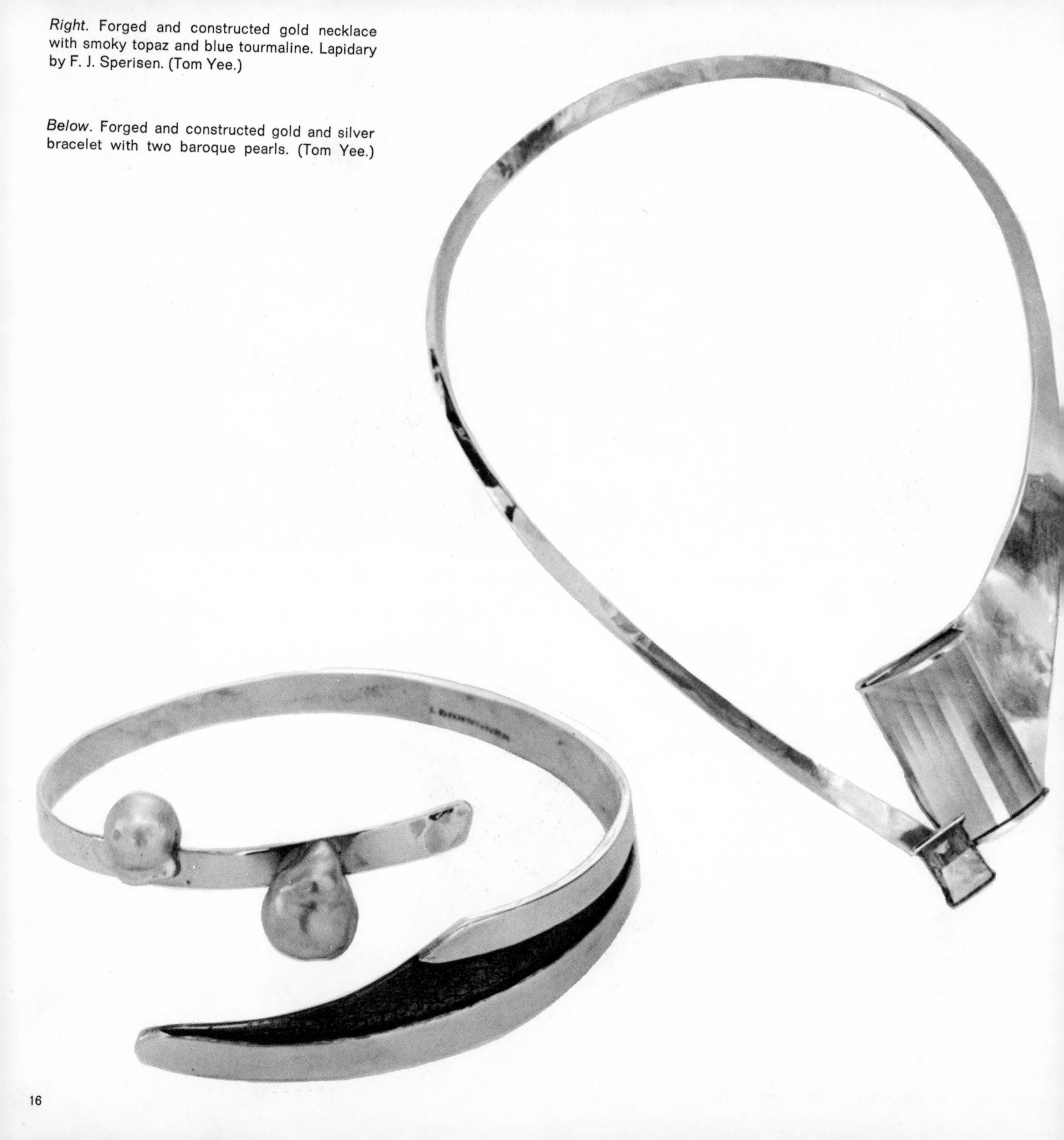

Right. Forged and constructed gold necklace with smoky topaz and blue tourmaline. Lapidary by F. J. Sperisen. (Tom Yee.)

Below. Forged and constructed gold and silver bracelet with two baroque pearls. (Tom Yee.)

Above. Forged gold watchband set with a smoky topaz and golden topaz watch crystal. Lapidary by F. J. Sperisen. (Tom Yee.)

Left. Forged 14-kt. gold necklace. (Tom Yee.)

Right. Ring of forged gold tubing with matrix opal. (Tom Yee.)

Below. Cast white gold ring set with a moonstone. (Tom Yee.)

Opposite Page

Forged and constructed gold hair ornament. (Tom Yee.)

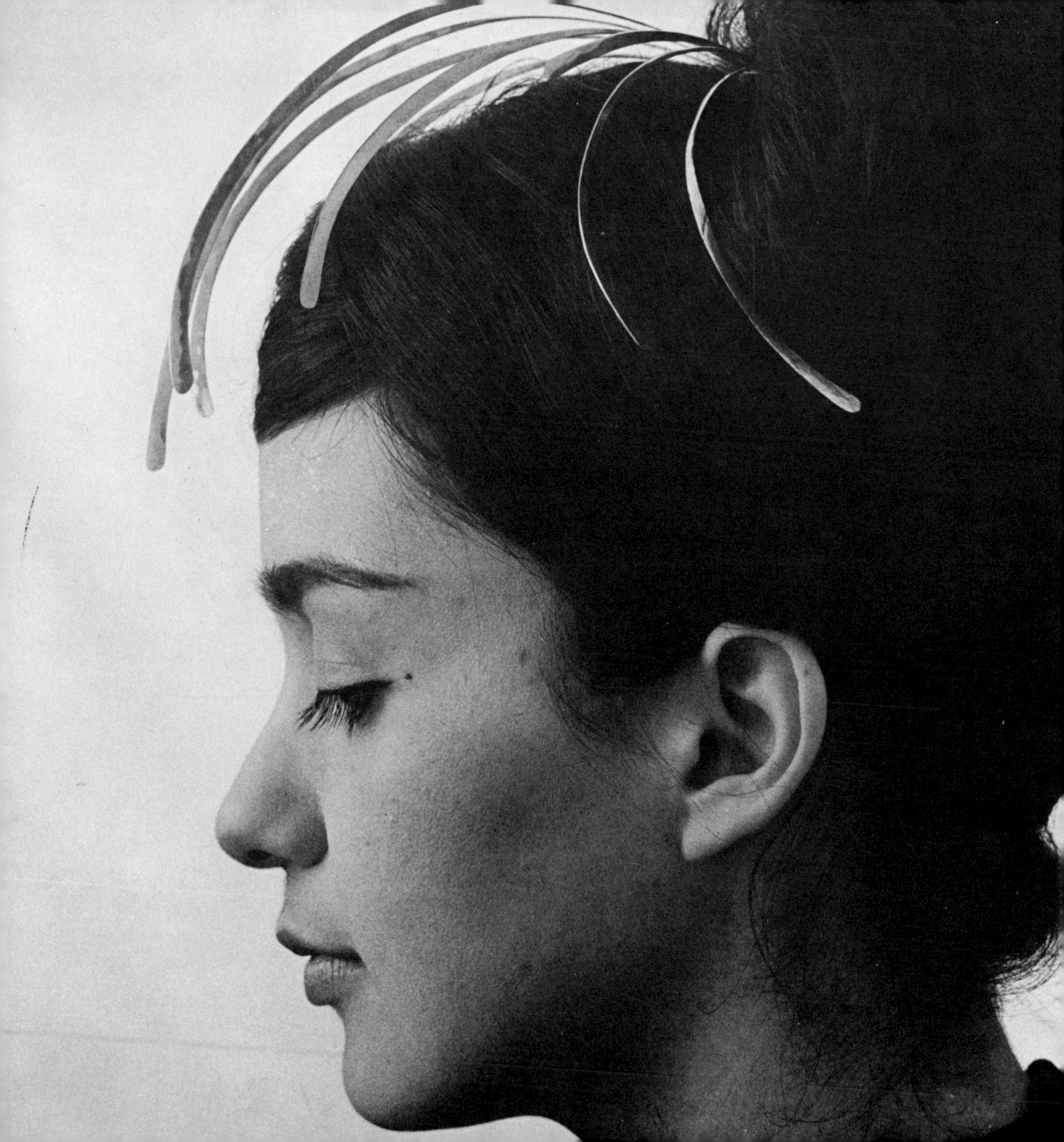

Constructed platinum ring with 32-kt. star sapphire and 22 diamonds (two views). (Tom Yee.)

Below. Constructed 14-kt. gold ring with a dark red diamond. (Tom Yee.)

Above. Constructed gold ring set with Wyoming jade and black and white pearls. Lapidary by F. J. Sperisen. (Tom Yee.)

Right. Cast 14-kt. gold ring set with jade and a black opal. (Tom Yee.)

my clientele in San Francisco was built up at those shows. Also, at that time, a group of San Franciscan jewelers headed by Margaret De Patta started the Metal Arts Guild organization, which resulted in one of the most satisfying and successful craft organizations I ever belonged to.

In the middle of my second year in jewelry, when I had about 36 or 40 good designs, I decided to make a catalogue for circulation among American gift shops specializing in contemporary designs. At this time a pair of earrings sold, wholesale price, for about six or seven dollars and I had to work at least 12 to 14 hours a day, seven days a week to make a modest living; but having to work under those conditions gave me the best technical training and practice that one could ask for. After the design problems were solved, the endless repetition of the same design allowed me to concentrate on perfecting my techniques: filing at just the correct angle; soldering so that the seam would barely show; bending silver in such a way that it would not have tool marks; polishing the fire scale—a gray film of oxides—so that not a trace of it was left; finding a way to make my oxidation, liver of sulfur applied to the metal, look rich and black. Because I had very little formal training in jewelry-making—just the bare essentials—my schooling consisted of endless repetitions and mistakes.

I recall one of my first commissions to make a ring and the disaster connected with it. It was a large, hollow ring, wide at the top and narrow at the bottom (see page 15, below). Over the ring base sat a well-fitted top of bent sheet silver with holes in its base for two pegs which were meant to hold pearls. Two parallel sides closed the space. I soldered on the top and then the side walls, creating a hollow space, closed except for the two peg holes. Then I cooled the ring, fitted the pegs and started soldering them in place. It did not occur to me that by plugging the holes, I had completely sealed up the hollow space in the ring. When the air in the space got hot and in expanding had no place to escape, it pushed outwards, forcing all my beautifully soldered seams

Above. Cast gold ring set with black opal and fresh water pearl. (Tom Yee.)

Below. Cast white and yellow gold wedding and engagement rings set with fresh water pearl and black jade. Lapidary by F. J. Sperisen. (Tom Yee.)

Opposite Page

Forged necklace, earrings, and ring set with Oriental gem jades. (Tom Yee.)

(text continued on page 27)

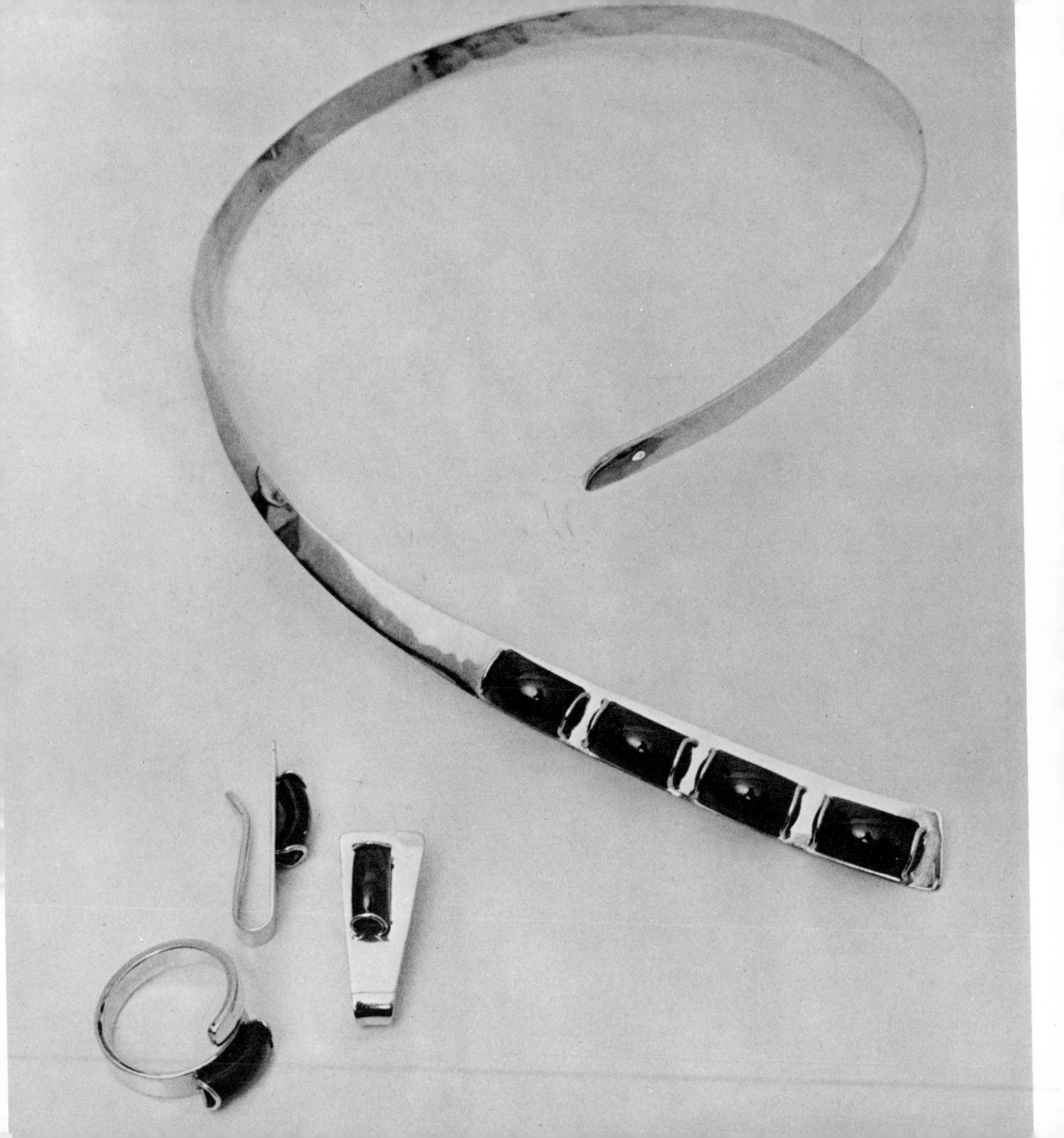

Left. Constructed and cast 22-kt. gold necklace with pendant of old carved jades. (Tom Yee.)

Below. Cast and forged 22-kt. and 14-kt. gold necklace with a detachable pendant of old carved jade. (Tom Yee.)

Left. Cast gold ring with marquise-cut amethyst. (Tom Yee.)

Below. Cast gold brooch textured with black sand and set with a wing pearl (original about 3 inches long). (Tom Yee.)

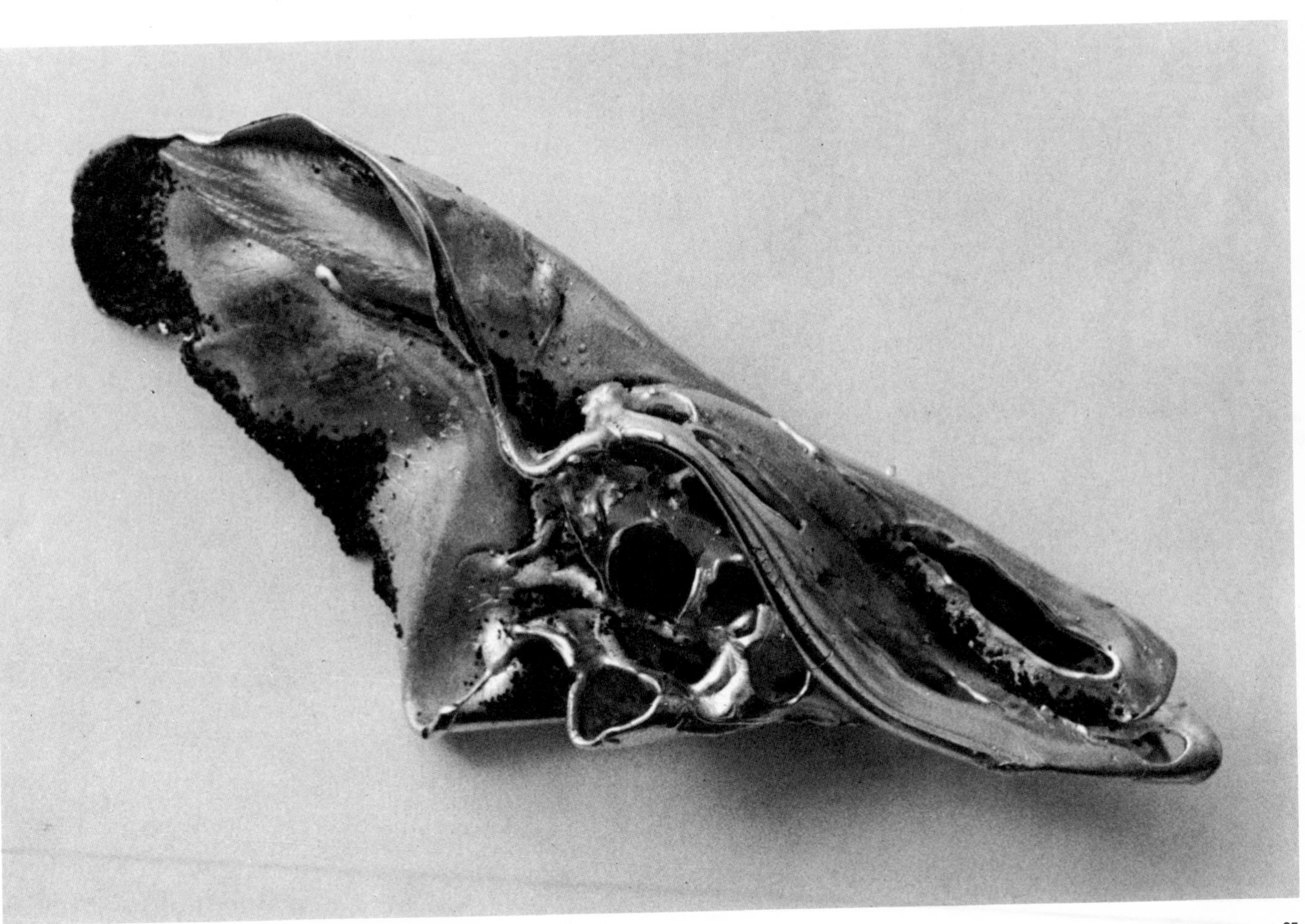

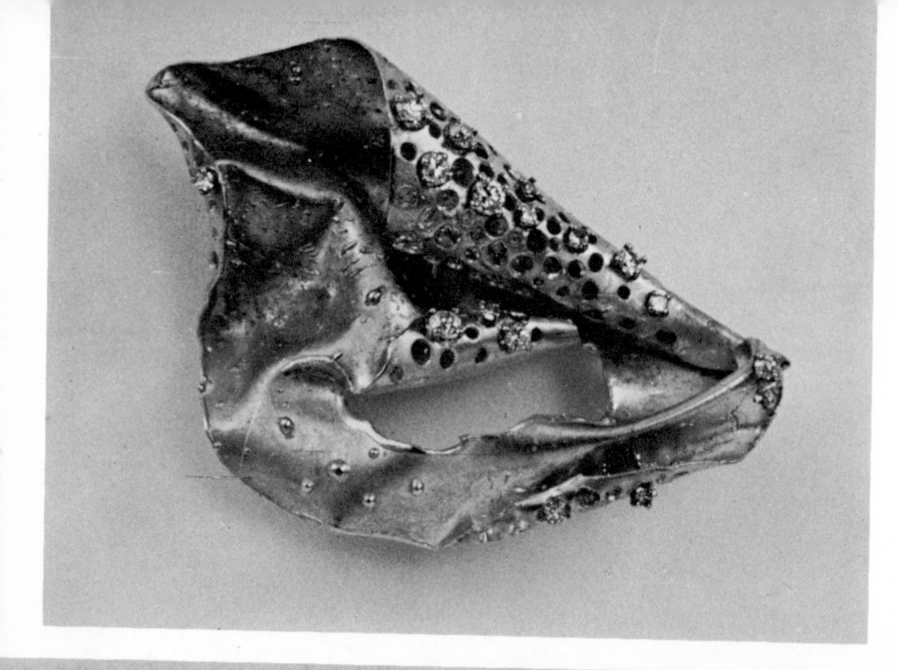

Left. Cast gold brooch with small diamonds (original about 2 inches long). (Tom Yee.)

Below. Cast gold brooch textured with epoxy and gold filings and set with jade (original about 2¾ inches long). (Tom Yee.)

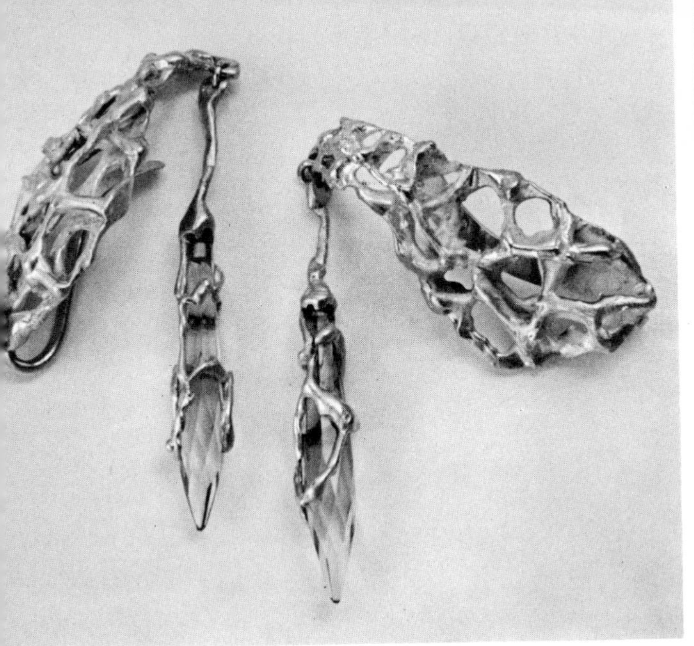

Cast gold earrings with topaz drops. (Tom Yee.)

Cast gold earrings. (Tom Yee.)

apart. I was stunned. I tried to resolder the seams, but only burned the whole ring up. Heartbroken, I had to start all over again. The second ring came out much better, and by trial and error I had learned a very important lesson—not to let hot air get trapped with no escape.

The process of wax-working, which I learned in arts and crafts school in Oakland, California, opened many new vistas for me, but I still had so many unexplored territories in straight metal-working that I used wax in very moderate proportion.

In 1952 or 1953 a group of us from the Metal Arts Guild got together and decided to have a seminar in silversmithing on large hammered-out, or forged, hollow ware pieces. That was a great experience. I learned how, in the process of forging, one can force metal to stretch or shrink.

I soon began applying this experience to my own jewelry-making. Although I had been making jewelry for five years now, I had hardly touched gold, and I will never forget how daring I felt when I first tried it. I took a foot-long, rather heavy square piece of 14-kt. gold wire and started forging. It was to be a flat choker necklace. When I finished hammering it, it was not very straight and was quite rough. I really did not know what the final result would be. How delighted I was to discover that it became like a spring; once I bent it into a desired shape, it would always return to it. I was able to pull it apart and open it up; as I let it go, it returned to its original shape. The necklace was a finished product, and a clasp was unnecessary (see page 17, below). This piece was the beginning of a series of asymmetrical forged necklaces. Later came a series of necklaces with forged sections which were riveted together. I began working more and more in gold. I found that my thin forged necklaces held their shape in gold much better than in silver.

At this time I arranged a one-man show in Hollywood, and for the first time, I prepared a rather large collection of gold jewelry. I had more confidence now and decided to try, also for the first time, expensive semi-precious stones. Despite all the hard work of preparation, the show was not a financial success, and a few years later I decided to try my luck in New York City.

I was already selling my things to Georg Jensen, and wanted to see if I could find additional outlets. In the spring of 1956 I flew to New York. Conrad Brown, an editor of *Craft Horizons*, introduced me to buyers in the stores that interested me, and to the directors of several galleries.

The reaction to my work was so favorable that I decided I must have a show in New York. Walker & Ebeling, Inc., a jewelry shop on Forty-eighth Street, agreed to give me a show in the autumn of 1956. They gave me some beautiful stones, including a 32-kt. star sapphire, a large tourmaline, gem jades, opals, and a ruby, and the freedom to do whatever I wanted with them. I made some of the pieces in wax-castings, but most of my work was forged or constructed. I prepared almost 60 pieces for the show—all in gold.

While in New York, I got a telegram from San

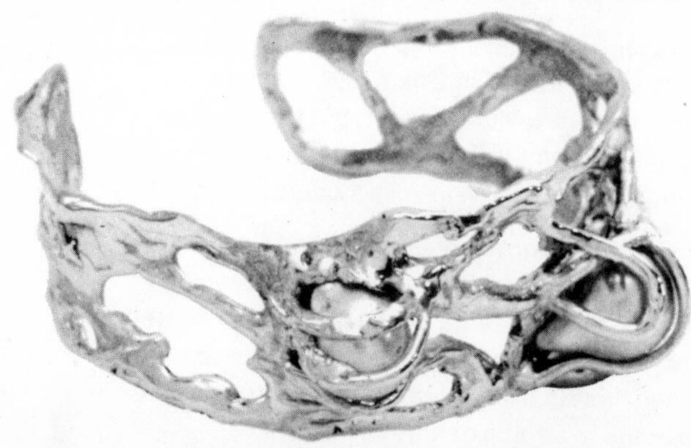

Above. Cast and constructed gold earrings. (Tom Yee.)

Right. Cast gold bracelet with baroque pearls. (Tom Yee.)

rancisco asking me to teach in the same adult ducation classes where, merely five years ago, I ad taken my own first steps in jewelry-making. I eturned to the West Coast, and three times a week or three-hour sessions, I taught 15 to 36 pupils in ach class. The position was demanding; the lasses were challenging and tremendously ewarding. Many came because they longed to work ith their hands, but did not believe they were apable of creating. Sometimes I nearly had to trick hem in order to prove to them that they had talent. Once they believed they could do something riginal, even if very simple, their imaginations

Cast gold ring set with emeralds and diamonds. (Tom Yee.)

Cast gold ring. (Tom Yee.)

Cast antiqued gold ring set with a 4-kt. Fabergé diamond. (Tom Yee.)

Cast gold wedding band with 64 diamonds. (Tom Yee.)

Cast white gold ring with South Seas pearl. (Tom Yee.)

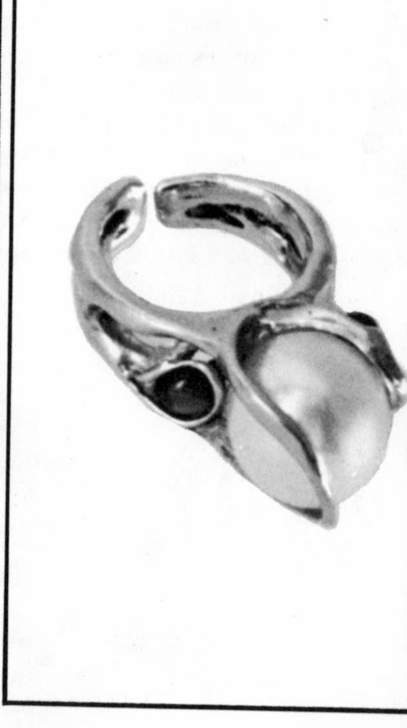

Cast gold ring set with a baroque pearl and sapphire. (Tom Yee.)

started working without any difficulty. A year and a half later, after I had moved to New York, I received over a hundred greeting cards from my pupils. I have kept them as the best reference I could have as a teacher.

I have learned much from my pupils. I had to think fast to solve all their problems; and all their problems were numerous and difficult. One cannot teach large groups collectively in a creative field. I am strongly in favor of individual instruction on the teacher-apprentice level. I believe a teacher has to help each student to develop his own approach to a design and his own way of solving his problems.

Despite the rewards of teaching, I still wished to

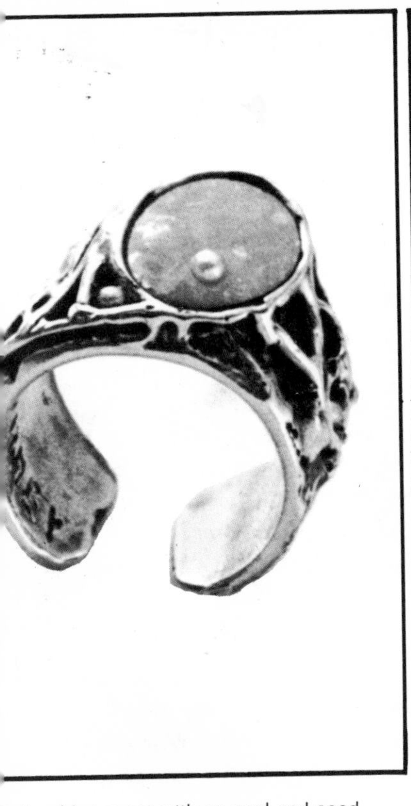

ast gold ring set with an opal and seed
earls. (Tom Yee.)

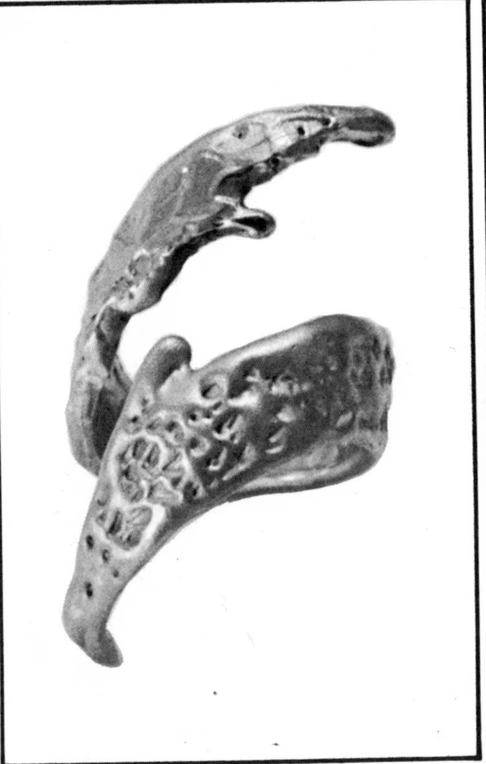

Cast gold ring. (Tom Yee.)

Cast gold ring set with a pale green tourmaline. Lapidary by F. J. Sperisen. (Tom Yee.)

eturn to the stimulation and possibilities for growth hat I felt existed in New York. My first one-man how in New York, at Walker & Ebeling, Inc., had een in October, 1956, but it was not until the ummer of 1957 that I was finally able to move there ermanently.

n my first year in New York I had many new experiences and ideas. That summer, The Museum of Modern Art had a large exhibition of photographs of the work of the Spanish architect Antoni Gaudí. It was a magnificent show, and one which impressed me even more than I realized at the time.

I have a theory that whatever surrounds an artist will be reflected in his work. Impressions of his

Cast 18-kt. gold ring set with amethyst. Lapidary by F. J. Sperisen. (Tom Yee.)

Cast 18-kt. gold ring set with an amethyst. Lapidary by F. J. Sperisen. (Tom Yee.)

environment filter through his subconscious mind and, in one form or another, come out in his art. This theory was unexpectedly confirmed when someone picked up my latest piece of jewelry and said that it made him think of Gaudí's architecture. The process of absorbing the impressions of that exhibit had been so completely subconscious that I had never even associated my latest work with that show. But after the relationship was pointed out to me, I had to agree that my work had the same baroque qualities which so impressed me in the peculiarly sculptural architecture of Gaudí.

It took me several months to get established in my work and in my new surroundings. Then I found that I barely had enough time to carry out all the ideas which were crowding into my head. I did not have a shop and worked from my apartment, and I had to build my whole business from scratch. Through The Museum of Contemporary Crafts, I entered a competition in which I won a place among seven other jewelers to exhibit our work in the American Pavilion at the 1958 Brussels World's Fair.

The influence of my new experiences in New York was making a very strong change in my work. I started to explore new techniques in wax-working. I began making lacy forms by piercing sheet wax with a hot tool and then blowing out the excess wax. Or, to achieve a different type of openwork, I dripped wax on a previously constructed mesh of wax wires. Either of these techniques in already cast metal can be reworked with a dental burr—enlarging the holes and making the walls thinner, resulting in still another effect.

In 1959 I had a one-man show at The Museum of Contemporary Crafts. It consisted of approximately 64 pieces, picked from work done over a five-year period. It showed a great variety of styles. There were very tailored forged pieces and very baroque, lacy, cast pieces. I never could stay with one style for any length of time. Even today, I do not have and do not want to have one stereotyped style.

(text continued on page 38)

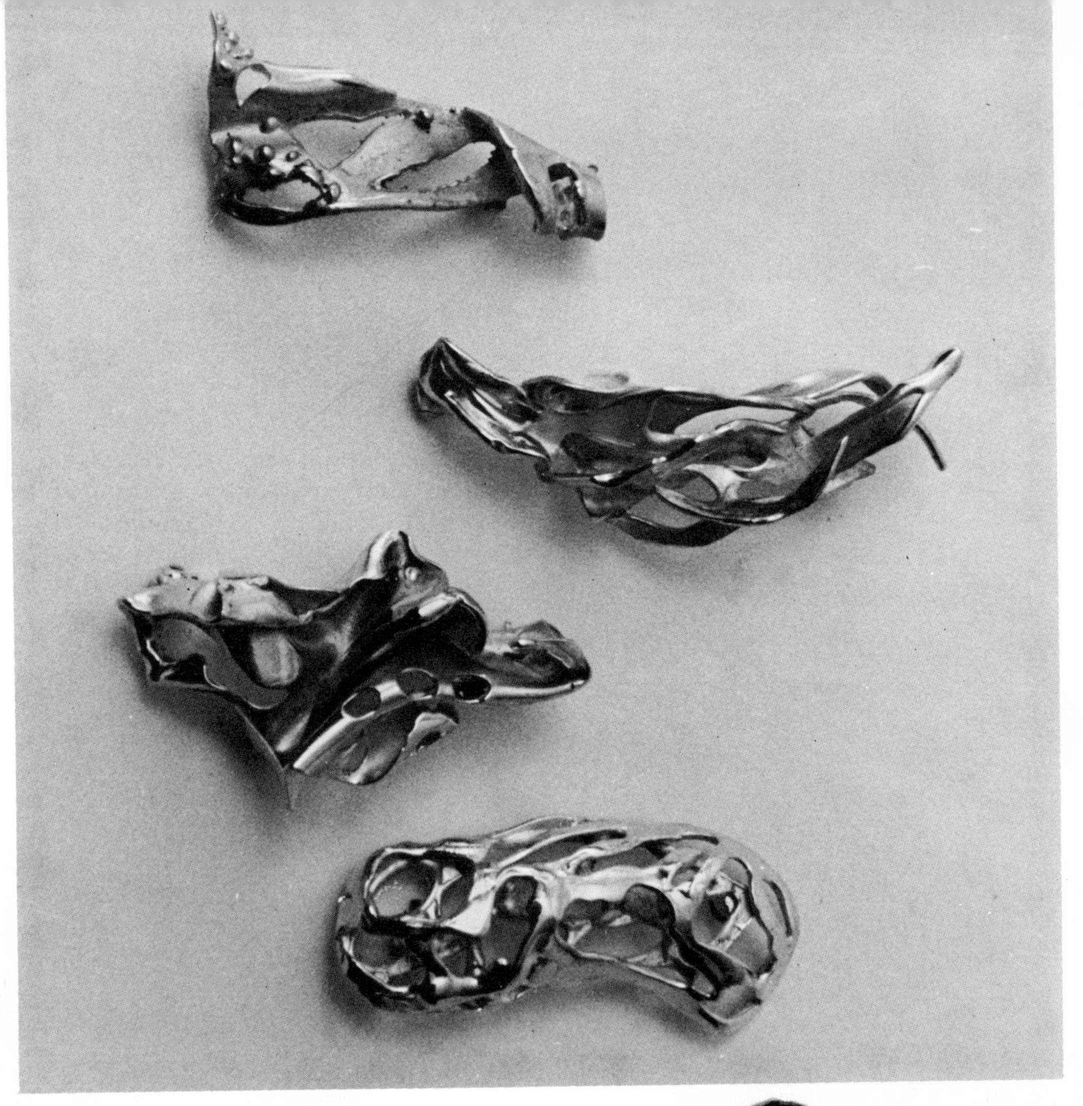

Above. Set of cast gold scatter pins (originals about 1½ inches longs). (Tom Yee.)

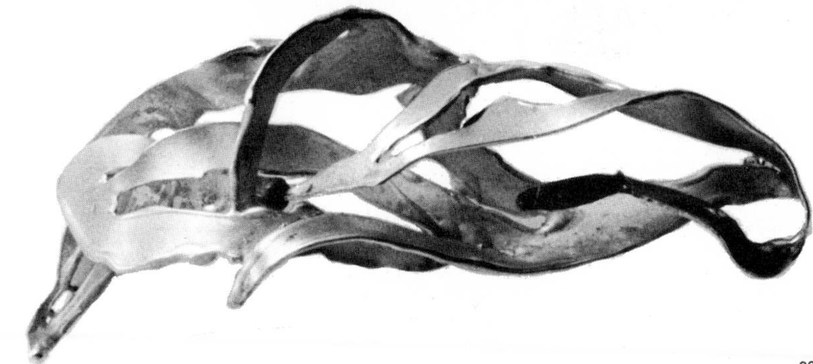

Right. Cast gold brooch set with ancient Egyptian faience beads (reproduced same size). (Tom Yee.)

Strand of pearls with cast gold decoration set with pearls, a star sapphire, and diamonds (greatly enlarged). (Tom Yee.)

Opposite Page

Set of cast scatter pins with various stones. (Tom Yee.)

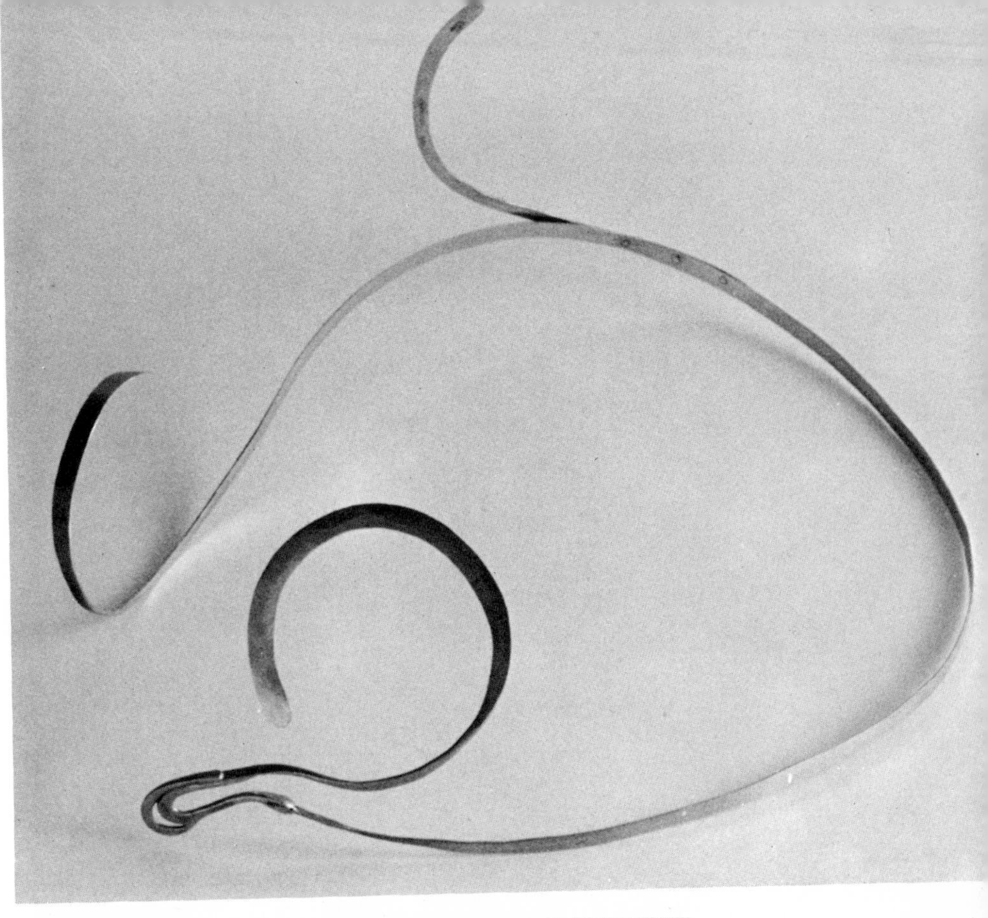

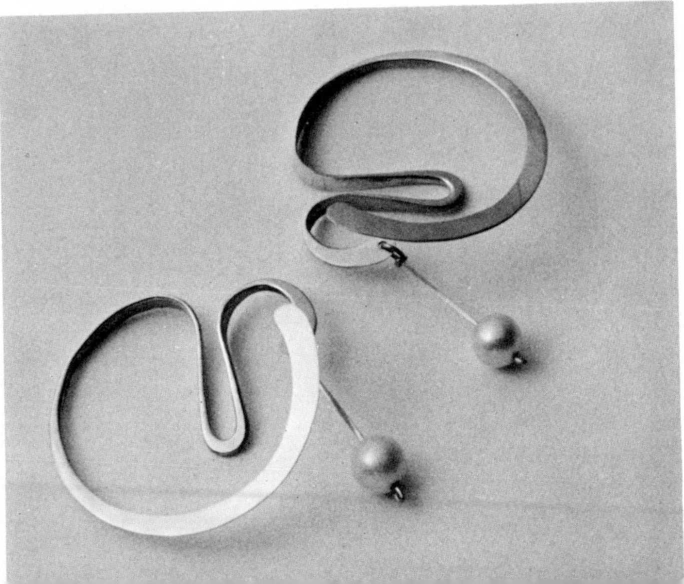

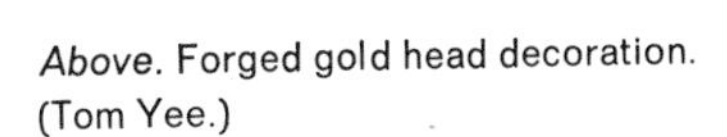

Above. Forged gold head decoration. (Tom Yee.)

Below. Forged gold earrings set with pearls. (Tom Yee.)

Opposite Page

Cast gold brooch set with a baroque pearl. (Tom Yee.)

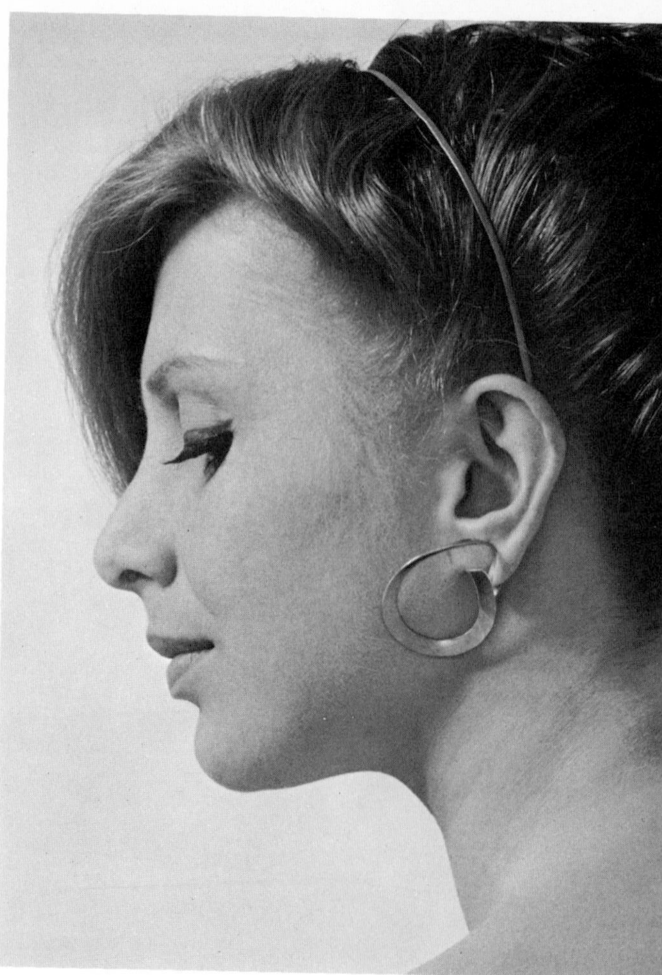

Forged gold head decoration with gold topaz drop (two views). Lapidary by F. J. Sperisen. (Tom Yee.)

Since 1959 my work has been exhibited in an international exposition in London; several times in Munich, where in 1963 I won a Bavarian state prize for a necklace; and at an international exhibition in Darmstadt, Germany, where one piece was purchased for the state museum collection. Today, I design primarily for individuals. I do not plan a style in advance, but try to let the style grow naturally from my impressions of the individual. I try to reflect as much of the personality of the customer as possible. The person should feel familiar and comfortable with the jewelry, as if it were a part of him. It should not be a mere decoration, but should become an integral part of the body. As architectural sculpture enhances a building, jewelry enhances a human being. In 1962 Leon Prebandier wrote of my work in the Swiss publication, *Architecture Forms and Functions* (Lausanne Kraft Edition, 1962-63, no. 9):

Forged and cast gold earrings. (Tom Yee.)

Forged gold necklace set with a natural emerald crystal. (Tom Yee.)

"In her workshop in New York, the sculptor Irena Brynner makes her jewels entirely herself. They are lost-wax castings. When there are stones, the settings are devised by following the shape of the jewel, a method that is far from the traditional mounting. The stones are sometimes sculptured instead of being cut in the classical manner. Often the gold, dull from the mold, is polished on its raised edges only. The jewel so conceived becomes a real play of light and attempts nothing more than to be an object mingling with life, thus finding its scale. The intuitive shape, spontaneously born from the fingers, reveals a long analysis of mankind by the creator, be that analysis conscious or not, and it is from here that the depth of expression has sprung. . . . Having made a very deep analysis of mankind, Irena Brynner has succeeded in a purely intuitive manner, in identifying the jewel with the individual."

Above. Cast gold necklace set with jade. (Tom Yee.)

Below. Cast gold chain with gold-colored oriental jade beads. (Tom Yee.)

Opposite Page

Constructed and cast 18-kt. and 20-kt. gold necklace set with jade stones (shown greatly enlarged). (Tom Yee.)

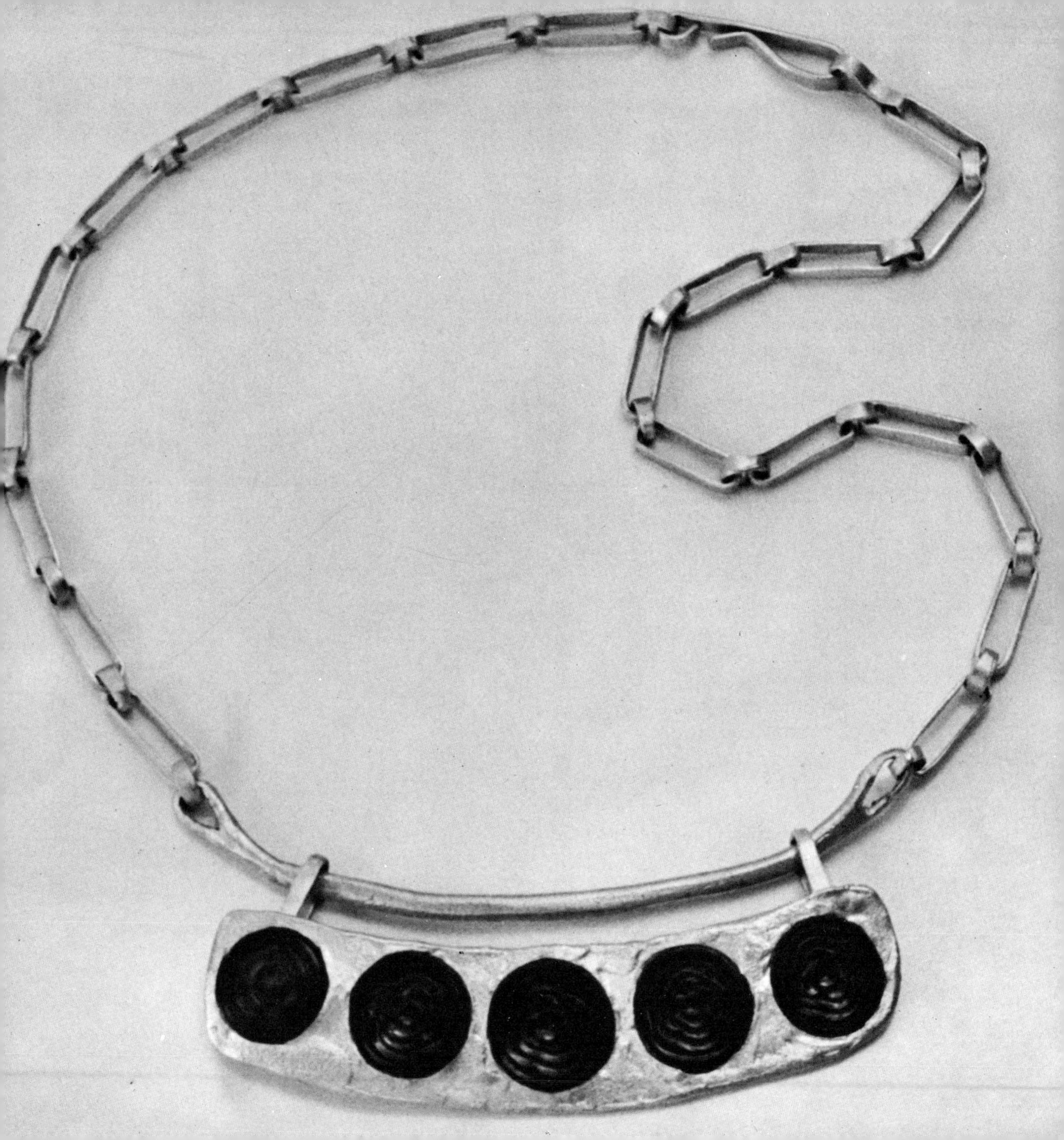

EQUIPMENT AND TECHNIQUES

CONSTRUCTED JEWELRY

When one is starting to work in metal and does not know much about its properties, it is best to begin with simple constructed geometric forms. Later, one's own development will create new demands for more sophisticated techniques. You will want to start forging flat surfaces into concave or convex forms. Later still, you will want to start on cast sculptured forms which can then be combined with forged forms. One never runs out of challenging problems, for they arise naturally in the course of experiment. Learning and exploring never end: the act of creation is always a miracle, and I never cease to marvel at it.

When making geometric pieces, start by sawing sheet metal into different patterns, sizes, and shapes. Some of these patterns may be bent, filed down, and fitted into other forms. When put together and soldered, they will constitute a three-dimensional figure. The sample drawing is based on a triangle, but other geometric forms such as squares, rectangles, and cubes are equally good to start with.

An earring of simple design can be constructed out of square wire. It too can be a geometrical form. In addition, the wire structure itself can easily be twisted, giving a rigid geometric figure grace and movement.

Tools.

Piece of rail used as an anvil, asbestos roll used for soldering, torch tip, ring mandril, snips or tinners used to cut sheet metal, small anvil, ring holder, steel anvil, hammer used for forging wires, saw frame, pliers and snips, half round file, tweezers, small needle files, chasing hammer, lead block, flexible shaft hand piece, bench pin, elbow support, buffs and burrs and drills for flexible shaft (on window).

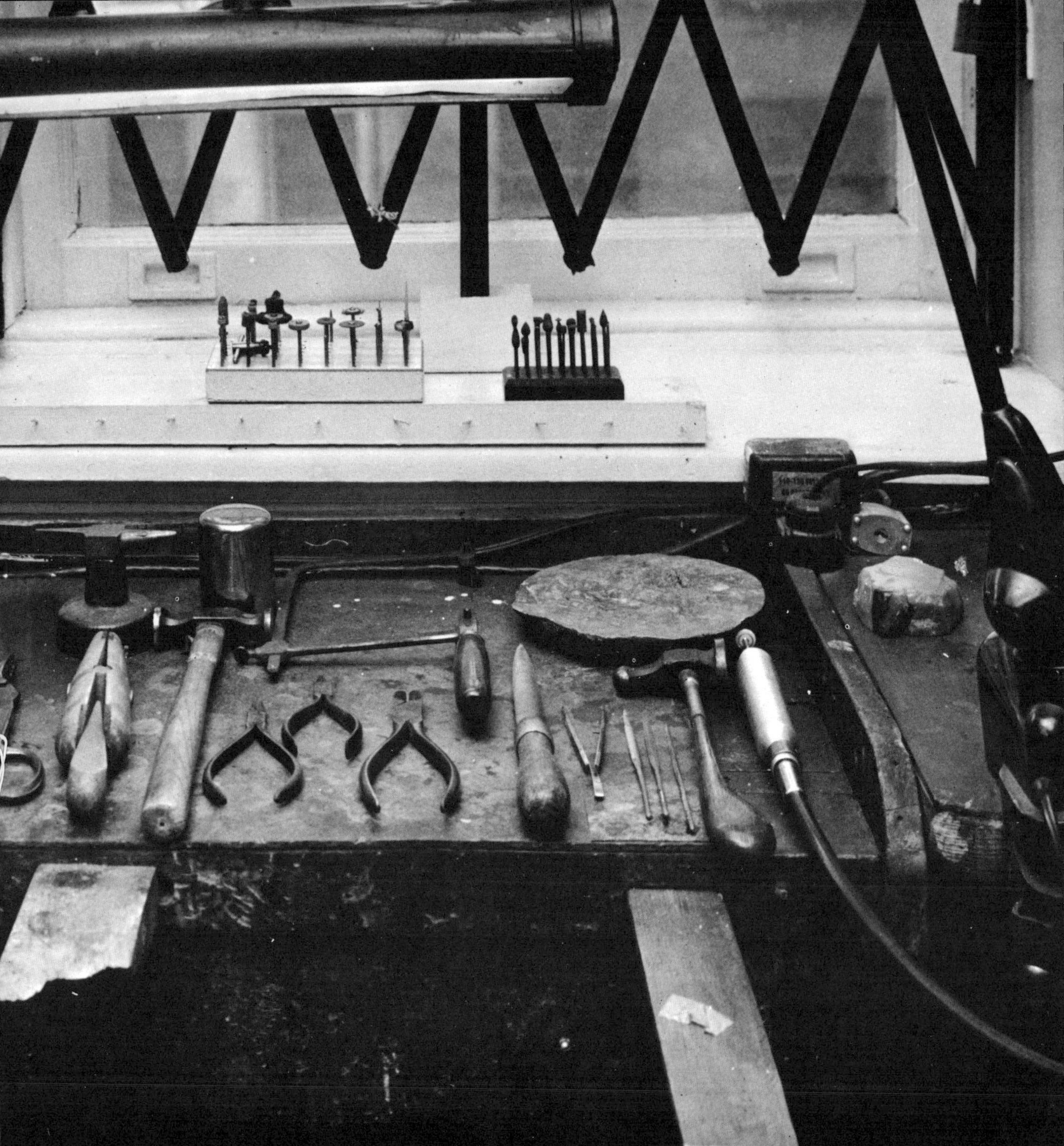

Constructed silver earrings set with turquoise. (Tatsuo Ishimoto.)

Opposite Page

Constructed gold necklace containing a fragment of an Indian cooking stone and set with diamonds. (Tom Yee.)

Constructing Cuff Link from Sheet Metal

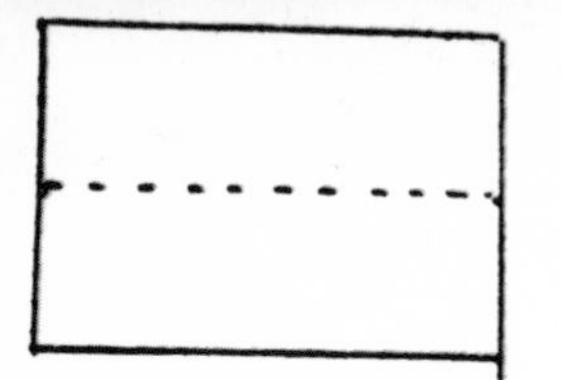

1 and 2. Two rectangular shapes are cut out of sheet silver, one larger than the other.

3. A decorative pattern is drilled on the larger rectangular sheet.

4. The larger sheet is bent as indicated by the dotted line (3), and the bottom edges filed so that the piece will sit flat on its base.

5. The bent form is fitted onto the smaller base, and the two forms are soldered together. A finding is then soldered to the base of the triangle, the piece filed and polished, and the result is a simple pair of constructed cuff links.

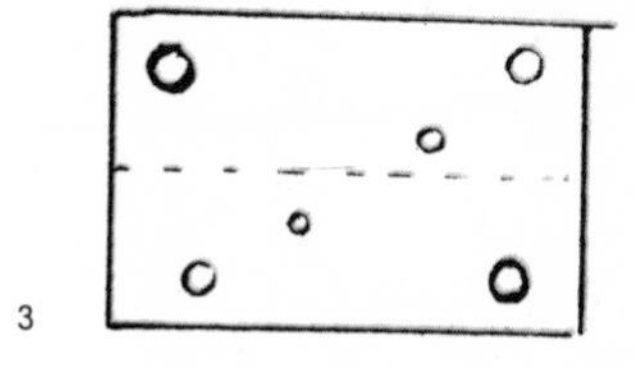

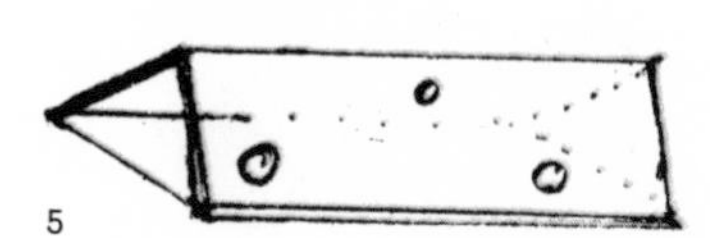

Constructed silver cuff links. (Tatsuo Ishimoto.)

Constructing Earrings from Square Wire

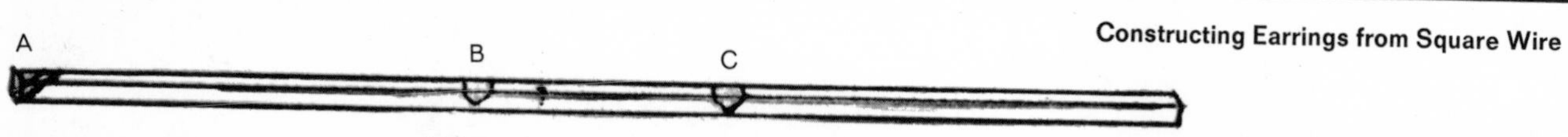

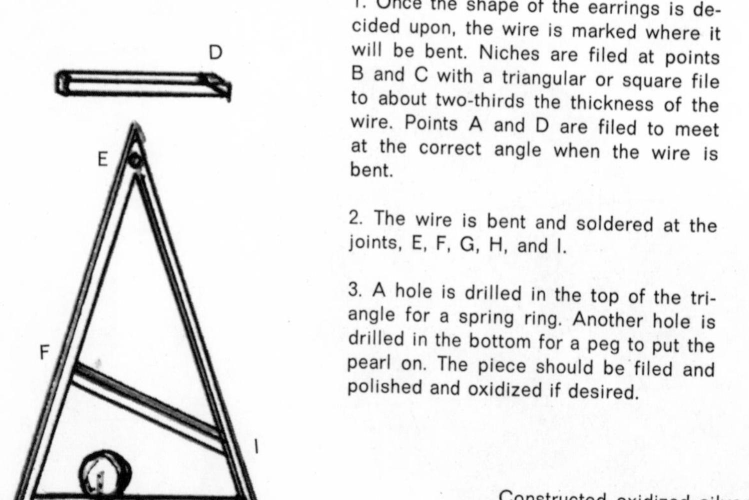

1. Once the shape of the earrings is decided upon, the wire is marked where it will be bent. Niches are filed at points B and C with a triangular or square file to about two-thirds the thickness of the wire. Points A and D are filed to meet at the correct angle when the wire is bent.

2. The wire is bent and soldered at the joints, E, F, G, H, and I.

3. A hole is drilled in the top of the triangle for a spring ring. Another hole is drilled in the bottom for a peg to put the pearl on. The piece should be filed and polished and oxidized if desired.

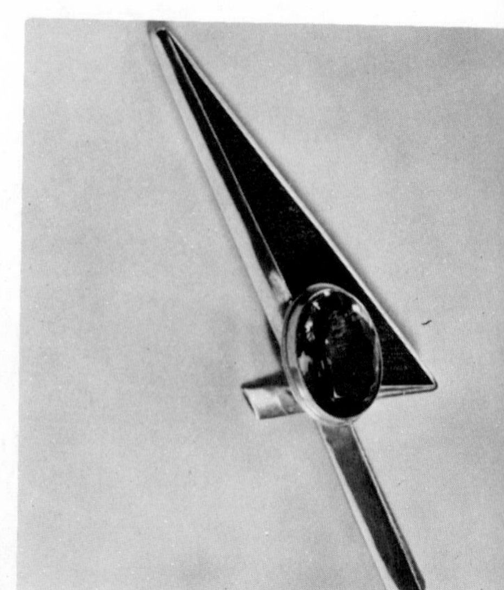

Constructed oxidized silver pin set with a topaz. (Tatsuo Ishimoto.)

bove. Constructed silver brooch and
arrings with stainless steel mesh.
Seorge Straus.)

ight. Constructed silver brooch and
arrings set with pearls. (Tatsuo Ishi-
oto.)

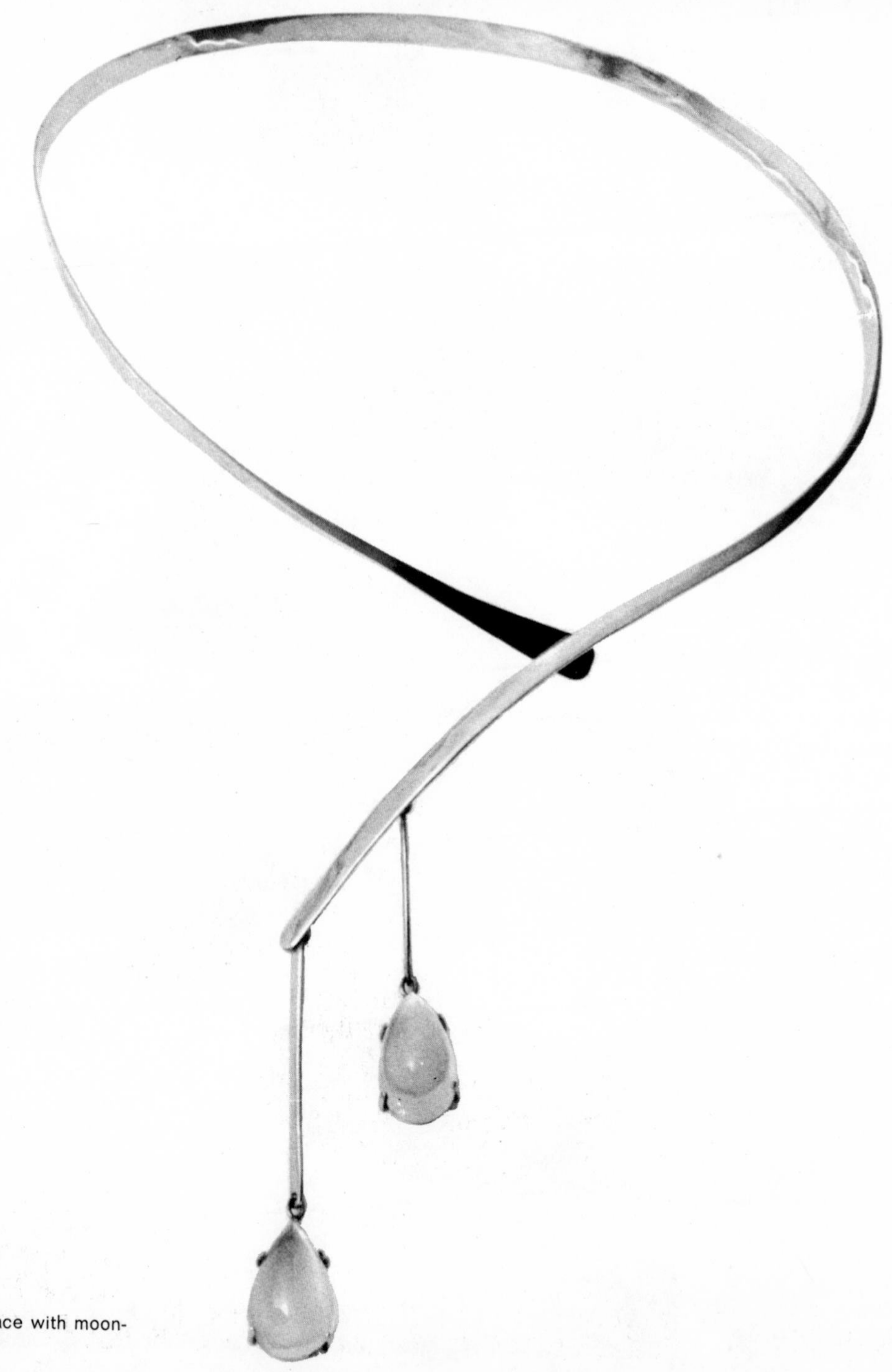

Forged yellow gold necklace with moonstone drops. (Tom Yee.)

ORGED JEWELRY

orging is hammering either wire or flat sheets of ıetal into a desired shape. To make a flat sheet oncave or convex, called "raising" the metal, the heet is hammered on a steel plate with a hammer ith a rounded head. Sometimes a lead or pitch lock, which are softer surfaces for smaller pieces nd more acute curves, is used to hammer on. If a mall curved form, like an indentation, is desired, is punched into the metal on a "dapping" block— steel block with various sizes of round indenta-ons. The sheet of metal is placed over the selected ıdentation and forced down into it with a ball punch.

orging changes the molecular structure of metal nd makes it hard and springy. If overdone, the ıetal becomes brittle and breakable. It must then e heated or annealed, restoring the original ıolecular structure and thus the malleability of the ıetal. By taking advantage of the elasticity of orged metals, you can make a necklace or bracelet ıat will always retain its shape. You will be able to tretch it or pull it open, and it will always return to s original curves.

A round silver disk is hammered into a shallow-domed form on a lead block with a rounded hammer.

Forged, domed silver pin with rutilated quartz sphere held by three prongs.

Wire necklaces can be forged in sections as well as in one piece. The sections are then joined either by riveting or by spring rings.

Different metals have different degrees of flexibility. Some are more malleable than others. Gold, for instance, gets harder than silver, has more flexibility, and conducts heat less quickly so that forged sections sometimes can be soldered together with little loss of spring. However, silver is considerably less expensive than gold and therefore a better metal to start with.

There is no hard-and-fast rule for forging. Practice alone will tell you when you have reached the exact degree of flexibility desired for the design you wish. You learn to "feel" when the metal is getting brittle and needs to be annealed.

Forging a square wire into a necklace. A round wire can also be forged using a steel block and a slightly rounded hammer.

Bending a forged-wire necklace.

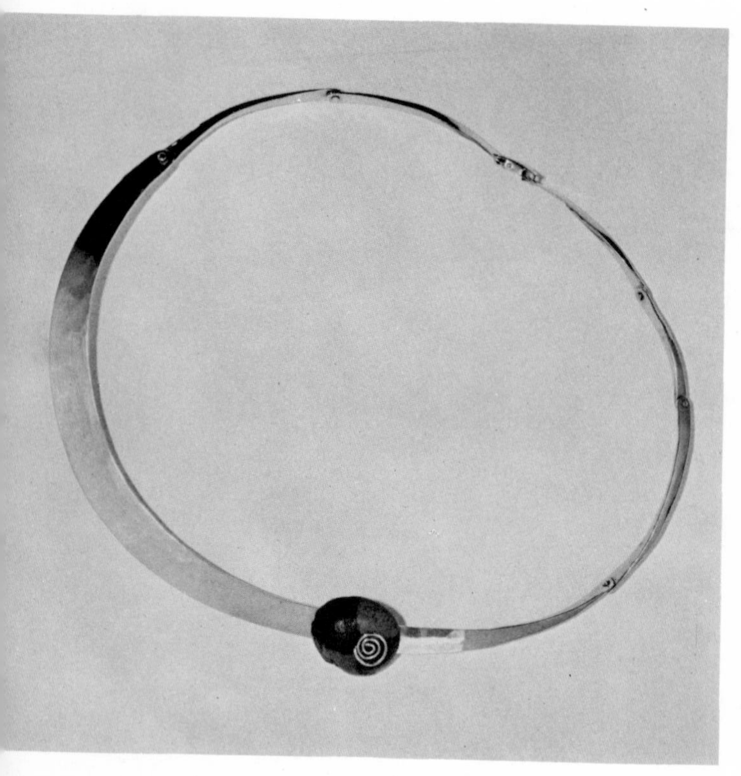

Forged and riveted sectioned gold necklace set with ancient Egyptian bead. (Tom Yee.)

Forged, sectioned gold necklace set with yellow and orange jade in a base of epoxy mixed with iron filings. (Tom Yee.)

Opposite Page

Forged and constructed gold necklace set with black opals of different shades. (Tom Yee.)

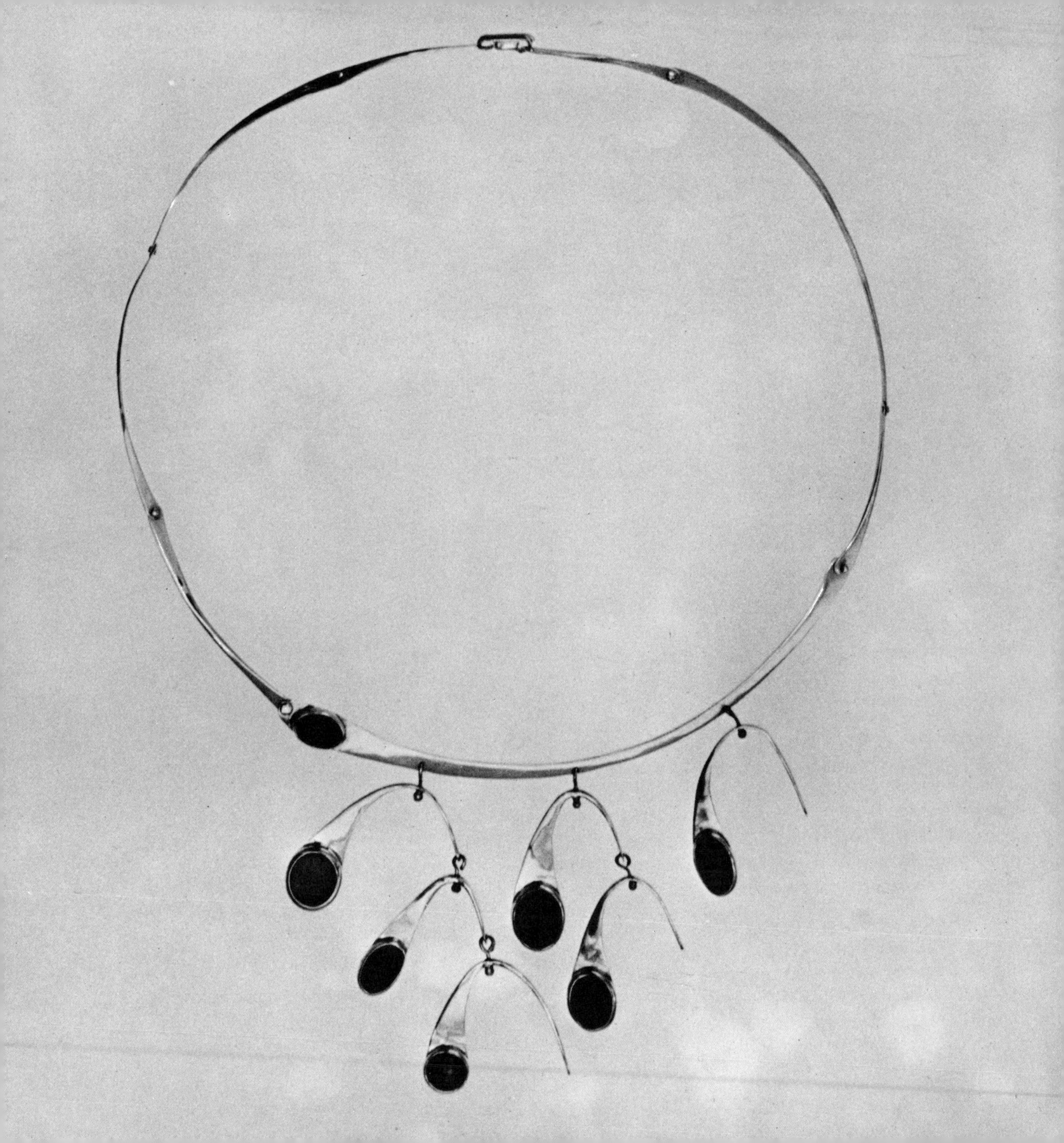

WAX-MODELING

To make simple sculptural forms in jewelry by building up forms in wax, you use basically the same techniques as for clay-modeling except that the forms are built up with drops of melted wax which are shaped with a hot tool.

Possibilities in wax-working are endless. One can use wax sheets of various sizes and thicknesses. Wires of all gauges are available and wax comes in dozens of different forms and consistencies. For example, there are soft, low-temperature melting waxes; waxes with a high melting point which are very gooey and stretch like toffee; and some waxes, such as Carvex, can be carved, filed, and drilled just like soapstone.

All wax's natural qualities and properties such as flowing softness and flexibility should be used to the fullest, making wax-casting a highly creative method of jewelry-making.

A sheet of wax, when warmed by a flame, can be stretched, bent, or crushed into any desired shape. It can be pierced or cut with a hot tool. Variety in the size and shape of the holes can be achieved simply by using different tools. When the wax has been melted by the tool, the excess wax is blown out—just as a candle is blown out.

The surface of the wax can be textured by scoring it with a tool, or by pressing it on some rough surface. Little granules of wax, their shape being controlled by the temperature of the wax, can be dripped directly onto a surface, thus building up a pattern.

If you wish to create a ring, it should be started on a form called a mandrel or, failing that, on any

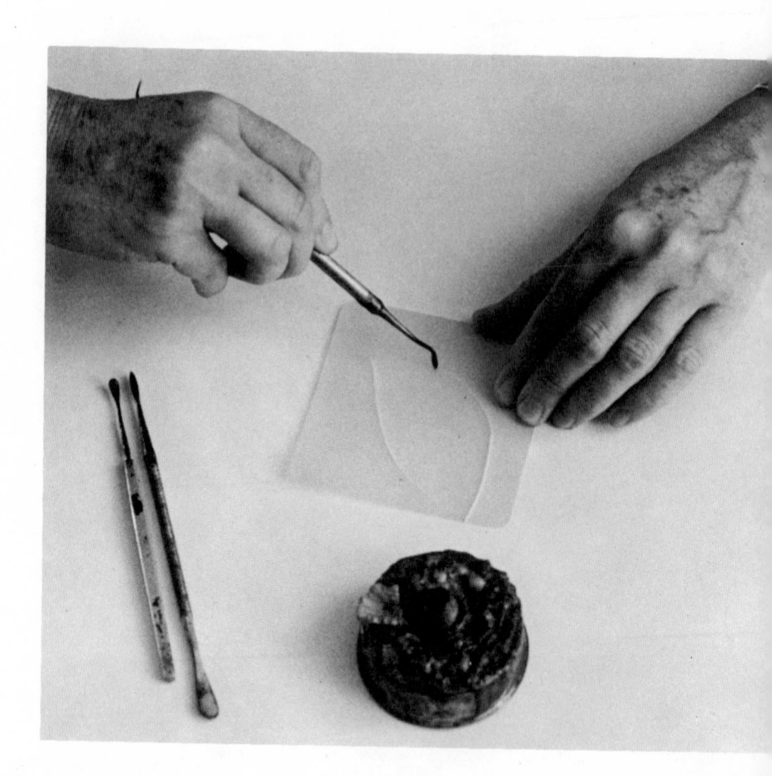

cylindrical form. Sheet wax or wax wires can be used to build up the base or band of the ring, and then forms are built over that.

If a stone is to be used it should become an integral part of the whole design. It can be secured on the ring in the desired position and then wax can be built up around it. To prevent the wax from sticking to the stone, it is moistened with glycerine. After

1 and 2. A shape is cut from a wax sheet with a warm tool. (The wax should first be warmed just to the point at which it is not brittle.)

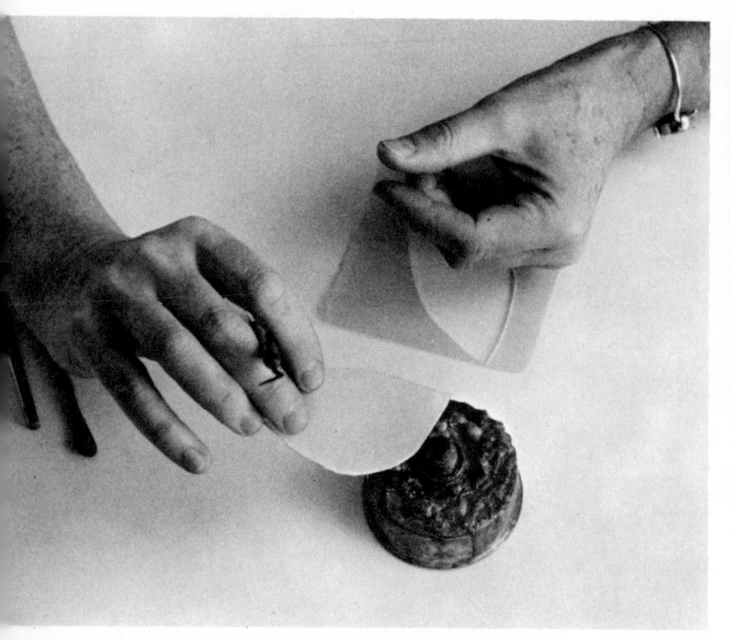

3. The wax is then warmed until pliable.

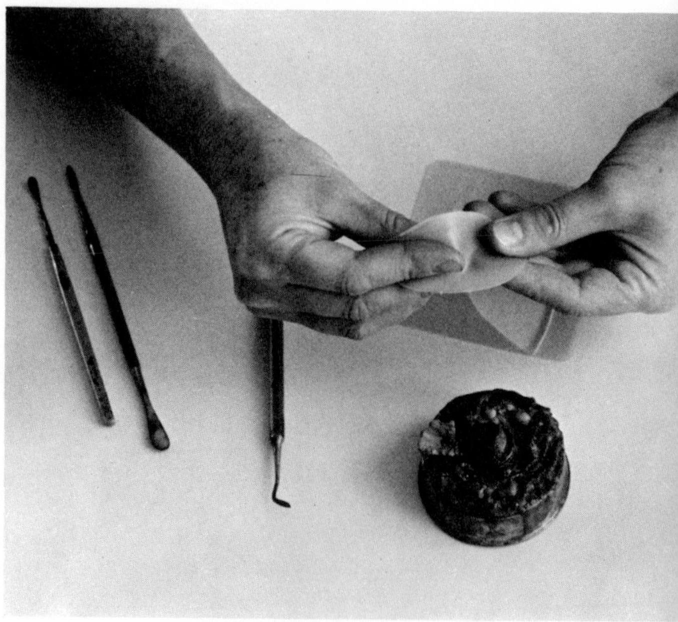

4. The warmed wax can then be molded into the desired shape.

the setting is finished, the wax around the stone is warmed so that it can easily be pushed out. The stone can then be removed from the setting. The ring should be cast in this open position, and only after the metal casting is cleaned, filed, polished, and the stone fitted, should you push the form back to secure the stone in place.

Carvex or any wax containing plastic can be stretched or pulled between two forms. This can be done by just holding a tool with melted wax near the existing form, and then slowly pulling it away at the precise moment of cooling, when it becomes stretchable. Only by practice can this be learned.

Forged and cast forms can successfully be combined by soldering. However, if the forged piece requires flexibility, one must be careful not to destroy it while soldering. Sometimes it is advisable not to forge the section that has to be soldered in advance, but rather to forge it after it has been soldered. The greatest joy is to discover your own way to achieve one or another effect.

5. The sheet of wax may be pierced with a hot tool to make a decorative pattern.

6. The melted wax is blown out of the pierced hole quickly, leaving a clean edge.

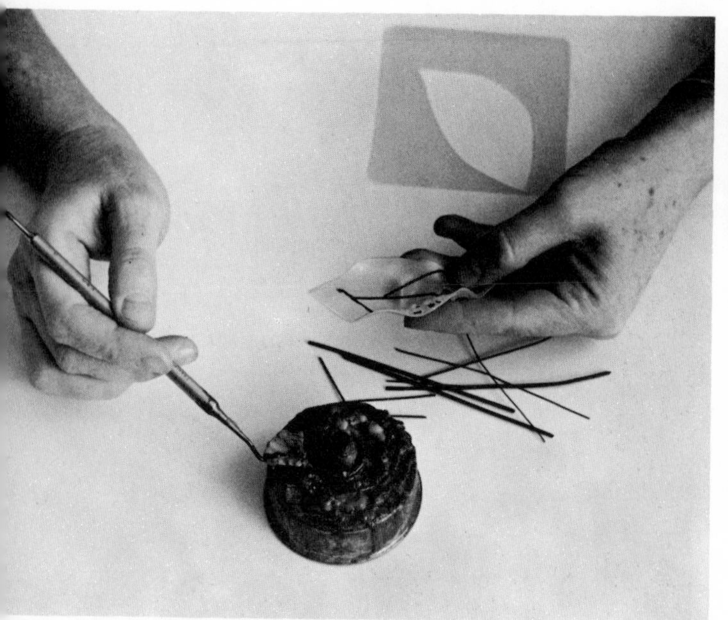

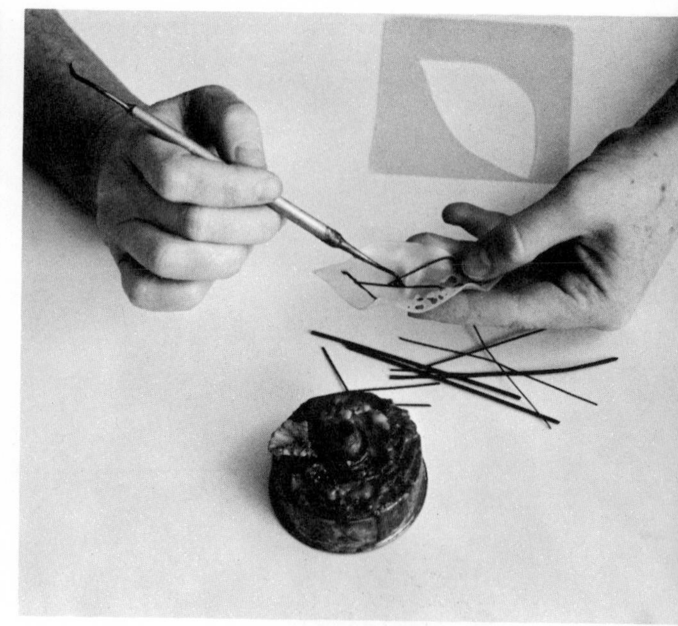

7 and 8. Wax wires can be added to the sheet of wax, giving variety to the design.

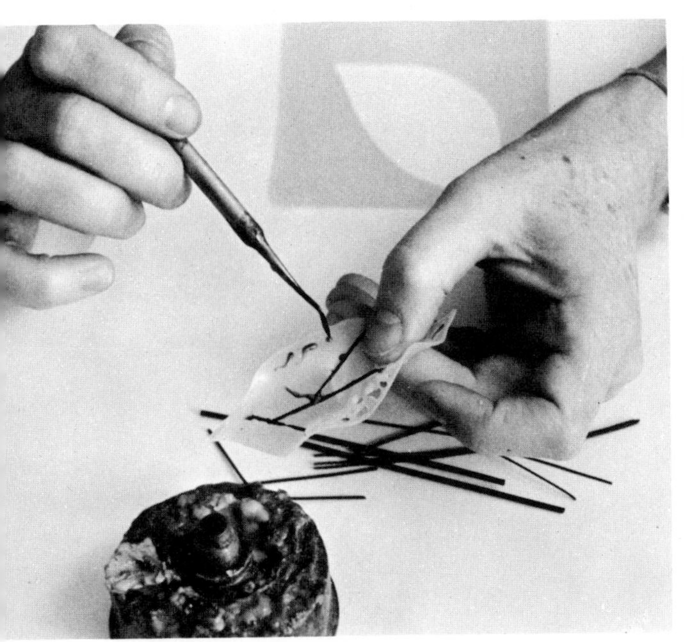

9. A relief design is made by dripping wax.

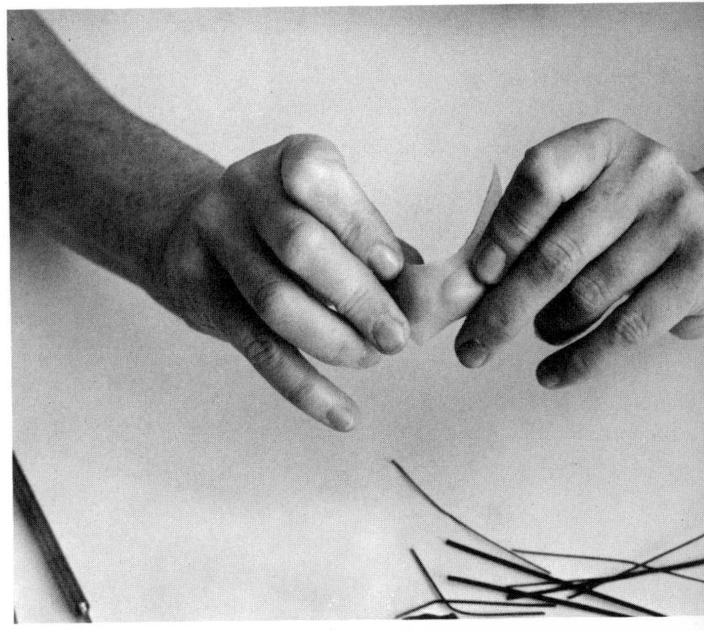

10. To create a domed form, a wax sheet can be stretched and molded when warmed.

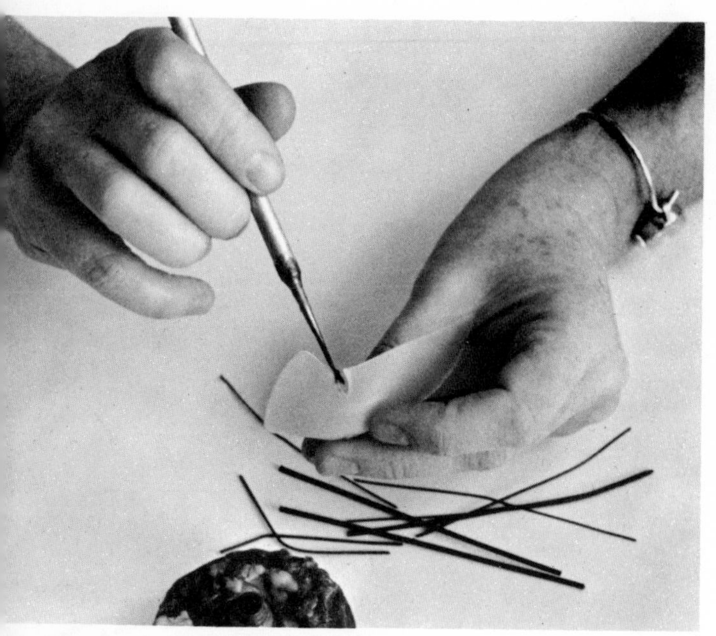

11. A cut in the side of the sheet with a hot tool prepares the way for making a domed form.

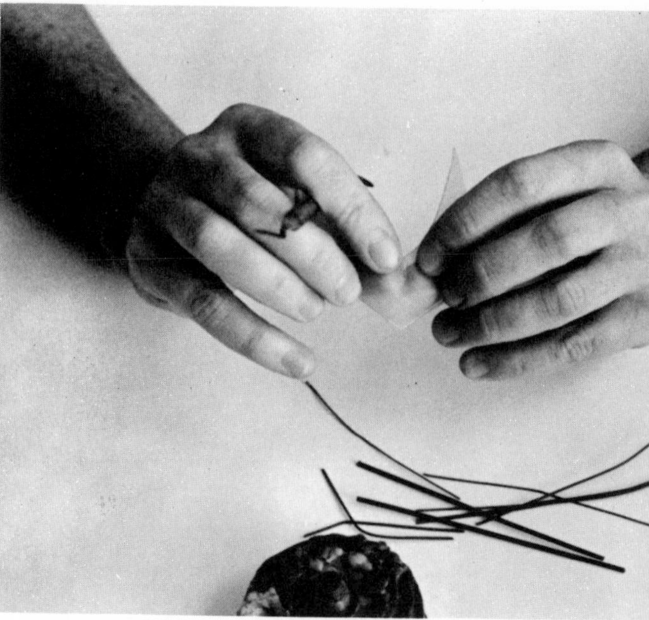

12. The two cut edges are brought together and welded with a hot tool, making a domed shape.

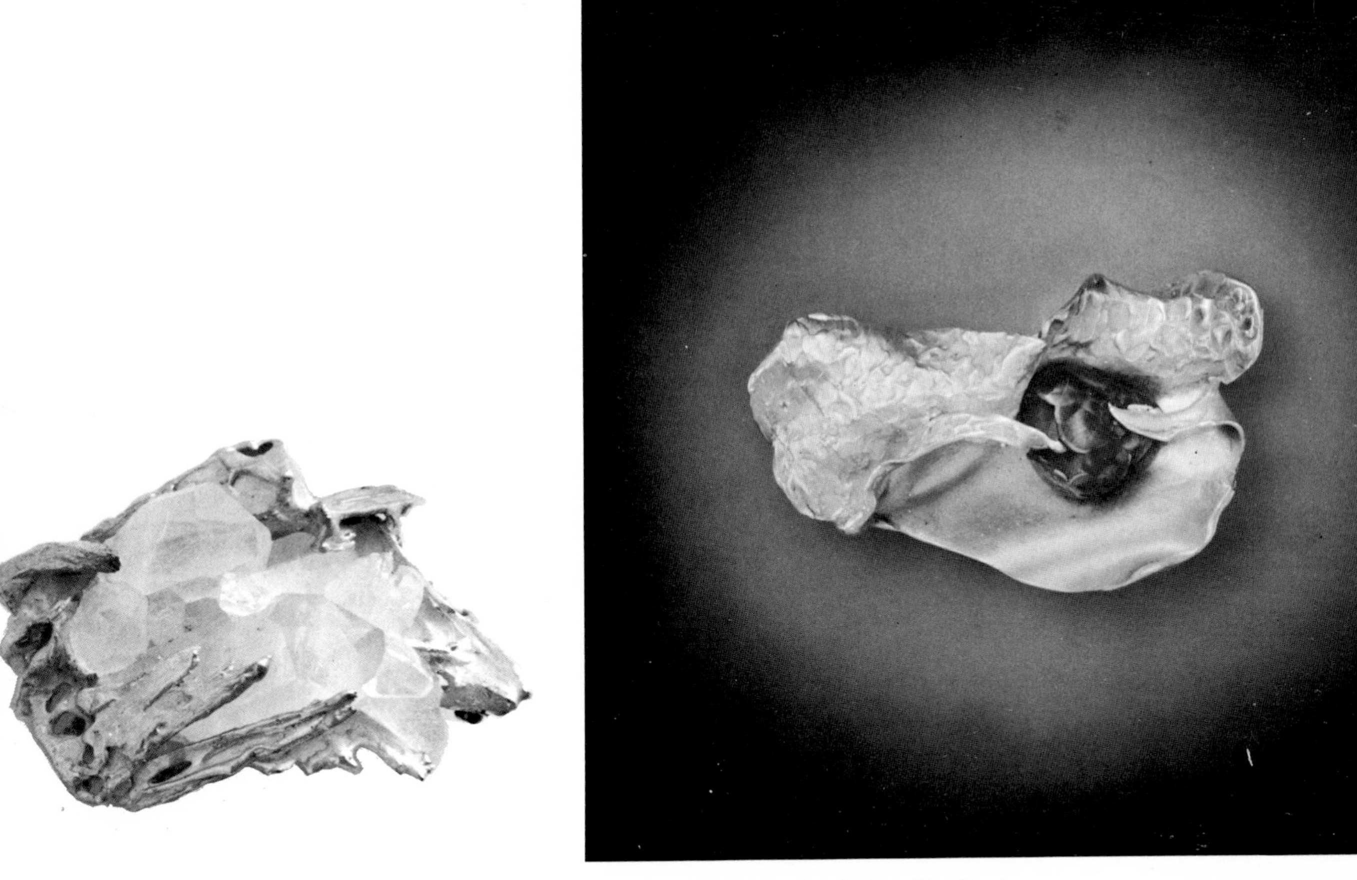

Cast gold brooch with natural rock crystal. (Tom Yee.)

Cast gold brooch set with malachite. (Tom Yee.)

Cast gold earrings. (Tom Yee.)

Above left. Cast sculpture of gold and silver. 5 by 6 inches. (Tom Yee.)

Above right. Red gold thistles with pearl mounted on beach pebble. (Tom Yee.)

Left. Daisy of malachite and jelly opal mounted on a green stone. (Tom Yee.)

Above. Cast gold wedding and engagement rings set with rubies. (Tom Yee.)

Opposite Page
Above left. Decorative cast gold comb textured with epoxy and set with freshwater pearls. (Tom Yee.)

Above right. Cast gold necklace set with freshwater pearls. (Tom Yee.)

Below left. Cast gold brooch set with green cat's-eye. (Tom Yee.)

Below right. Cast gold brooch set with emeralds. (Tom Yee.)

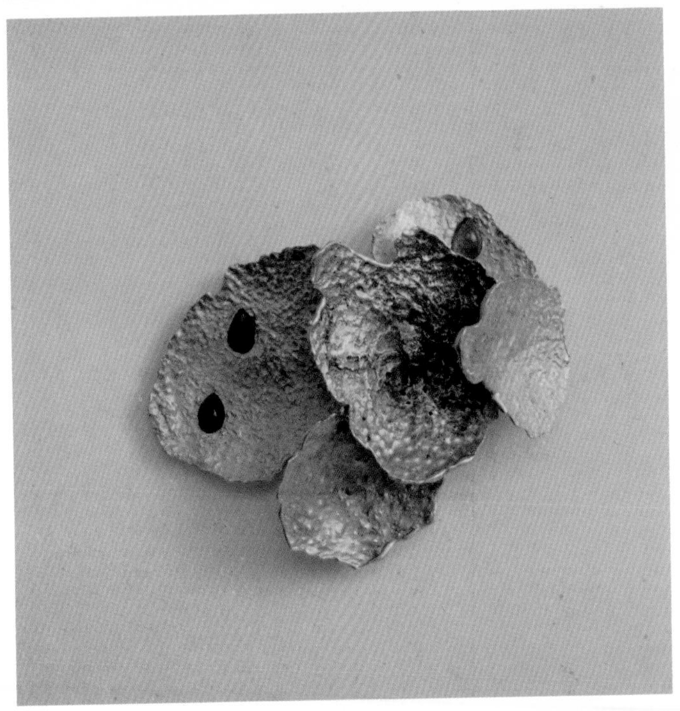

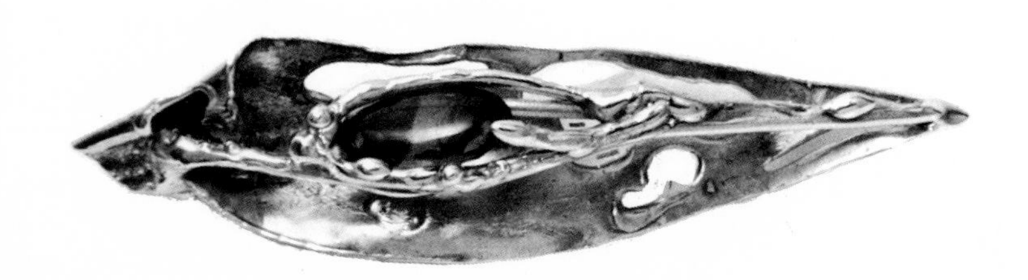

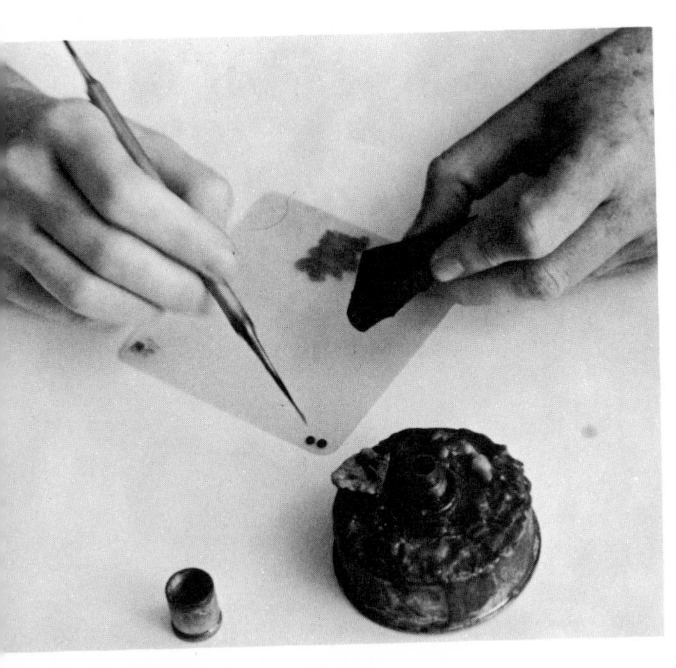

1. Achieving different textures with wax. Little drops of wax can be dripped from a hot tool onto a sheet of wax. The hotter the temperature of the wax, the flatter the shape of the droplet will be. Round drops are achieved by letting the wax cool first.

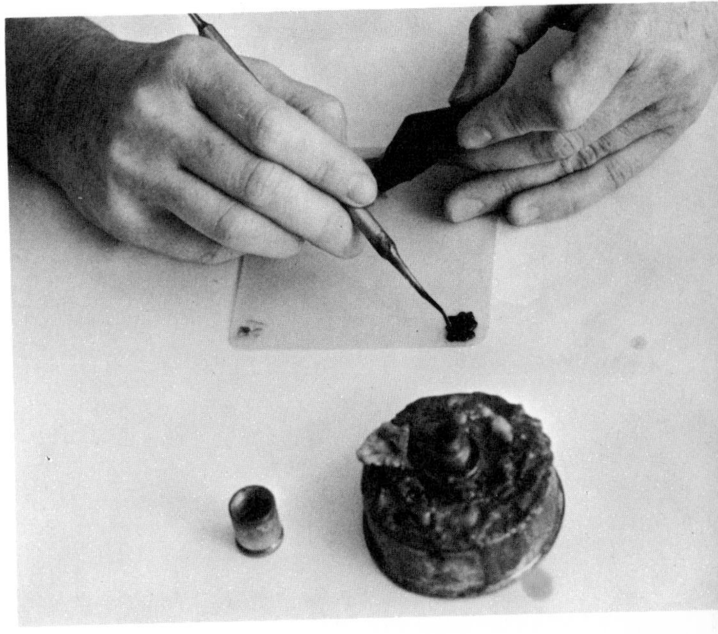

2. Wax drops can be used to build up forms.

Opposite Page

Top. Cast gold brooch set with a gold topaz. Lapidary by F. J. Sperisen. (Tom Yee.)

Center. Cast green gold brooch set with a jelly opal and textured with epoxy mixed with iron filings. (Tom Yee.)

Bottom. Cast gold brooch set with an amethyst. (Tom Yee.)

3. Soft wax can be smeared across a surface of hard wax to create streaks.

4. Different shapes can be achieved by dripping wax into water.

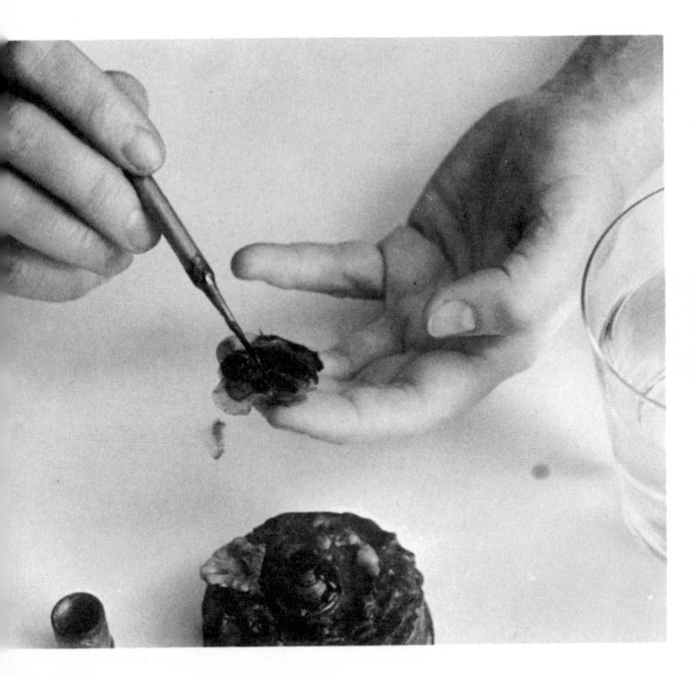

5. The hardened wax droplets are then put together in a pattern.

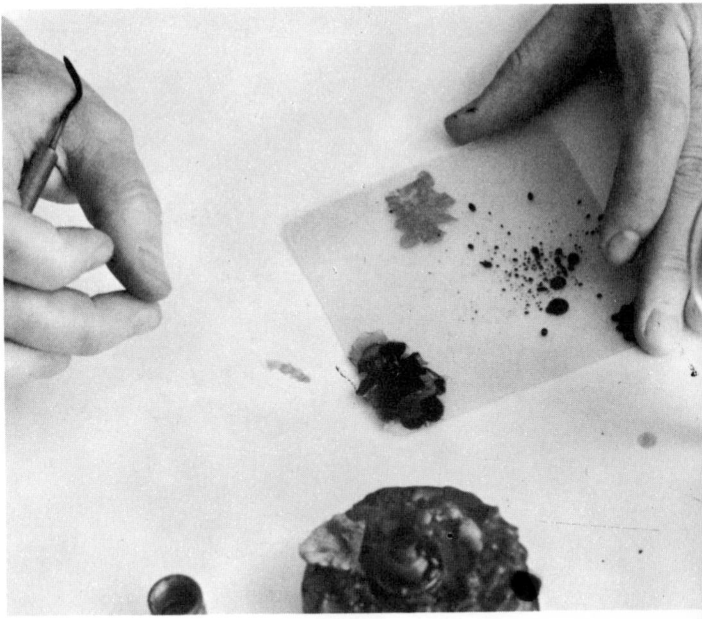

6. Wax can be blown on surfaces to create a splashed effect.

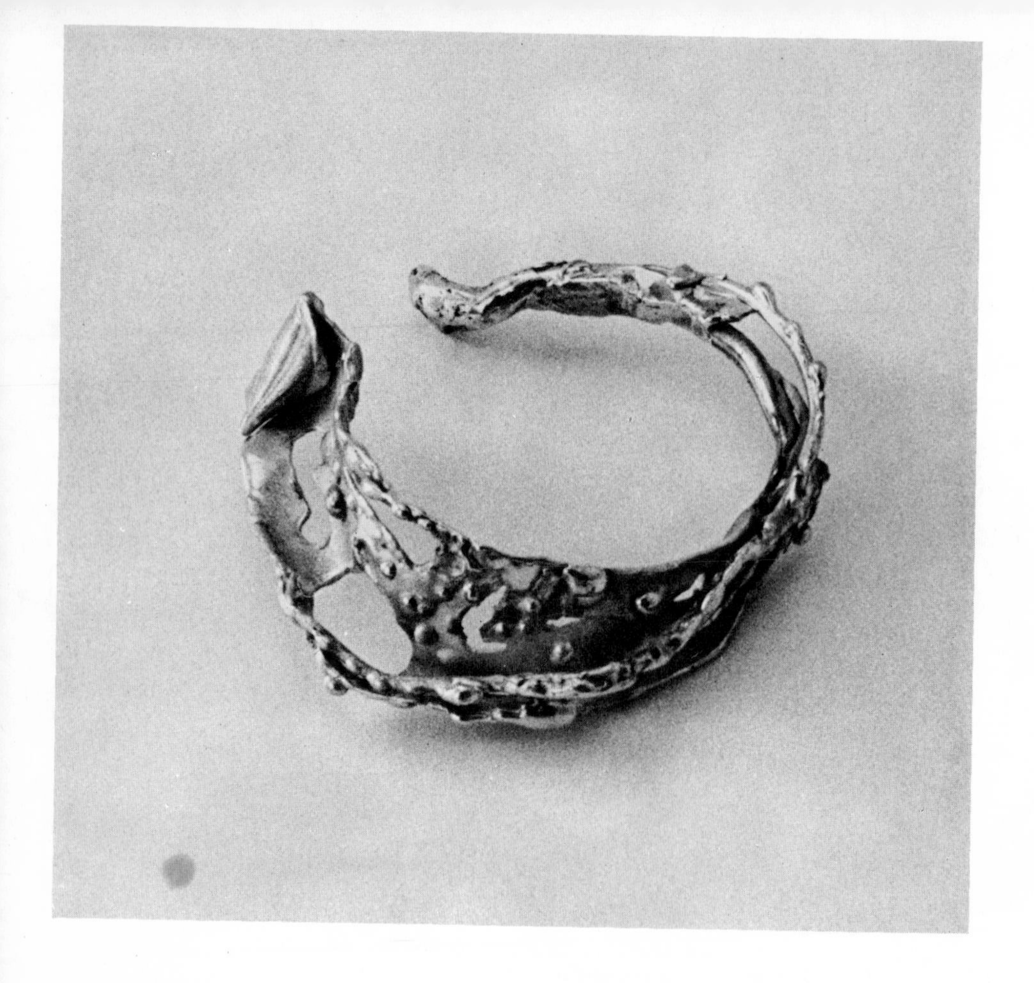

Above. Cast gold bracelet. (Tom Yee.)

Opposite Page

Cast gold bangle bracelets. (Tom Yee.)

BUILDING A RING

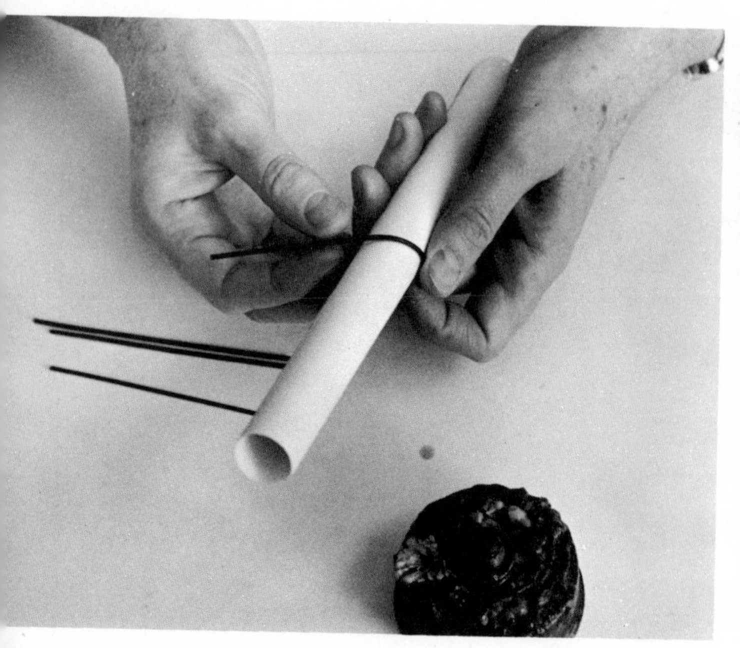

1. Wax wires are shaped around a mandrel.

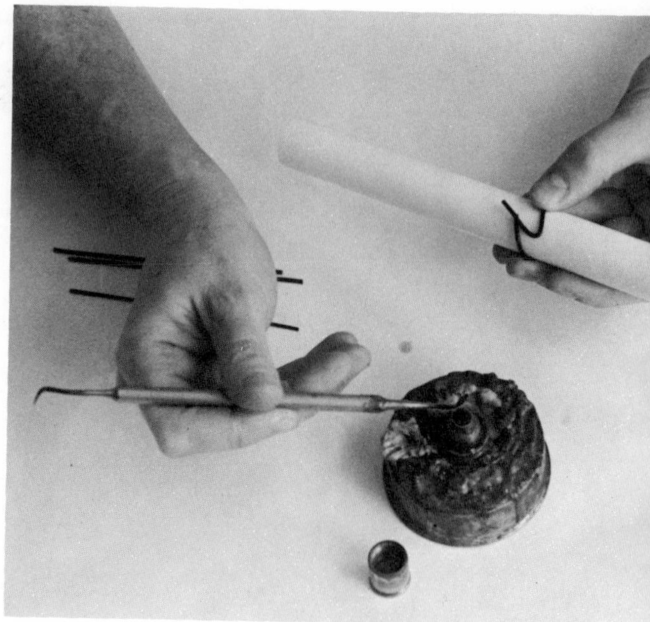

2. The ends of the wires are joined and sealed with a hot tool, and the excess wire is trimmed off.

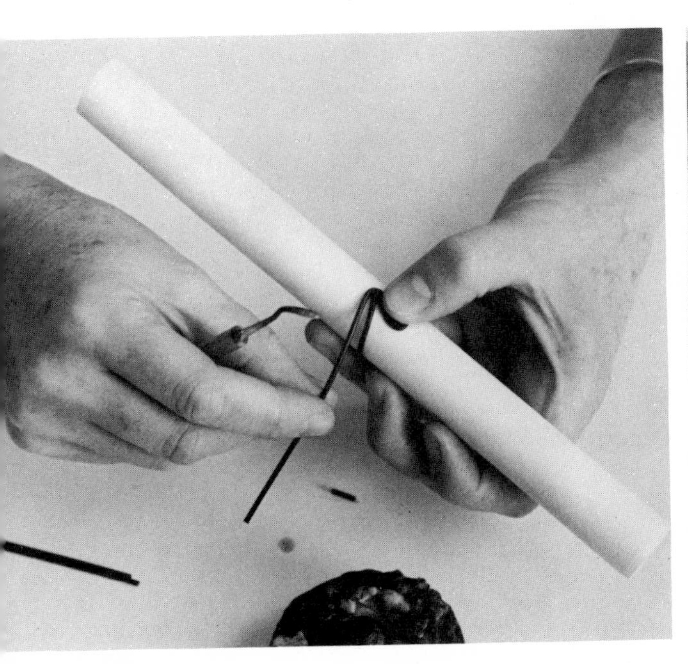

3. A second wax wire is shaped next to the first one.

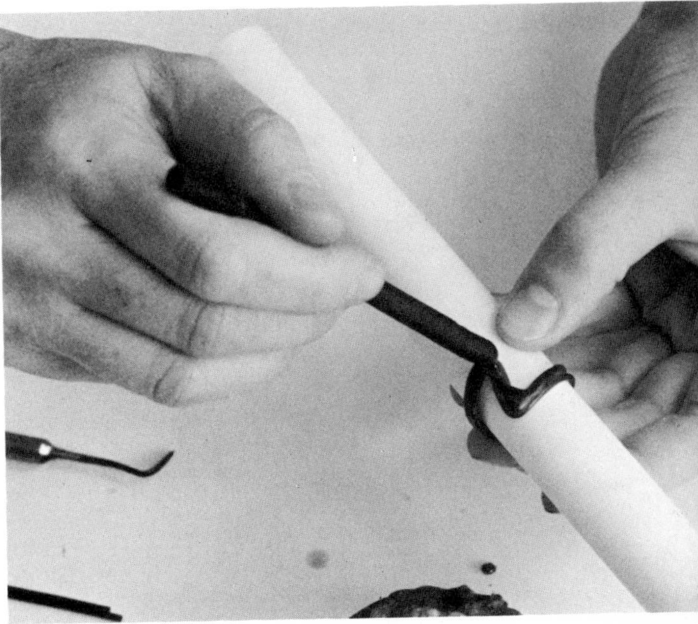

4. A hot wax rod is used to build up the thickness of the ring.

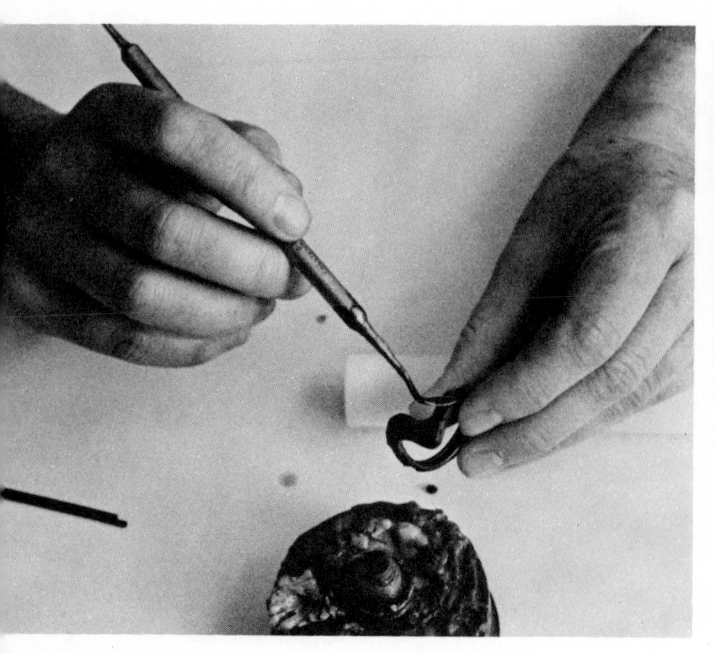

5. The form of the ring is smoothed and shaped with a tool.

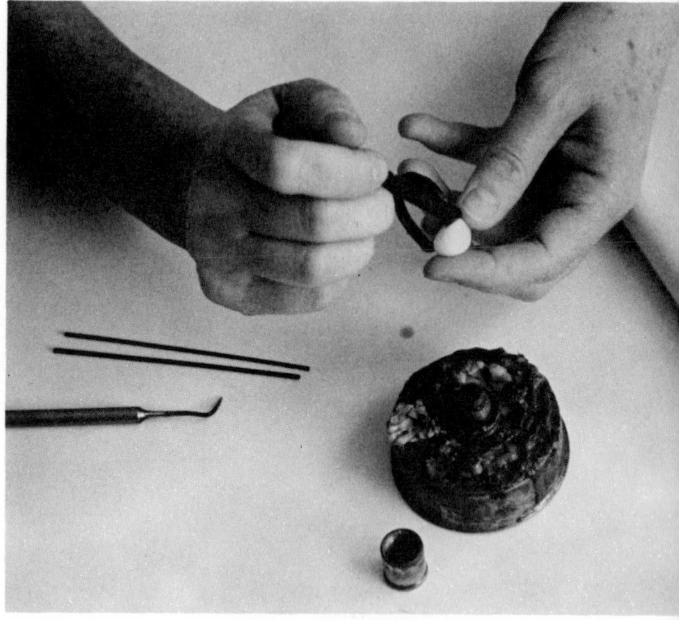

6. A stone is put in place with a bit of melted wax.

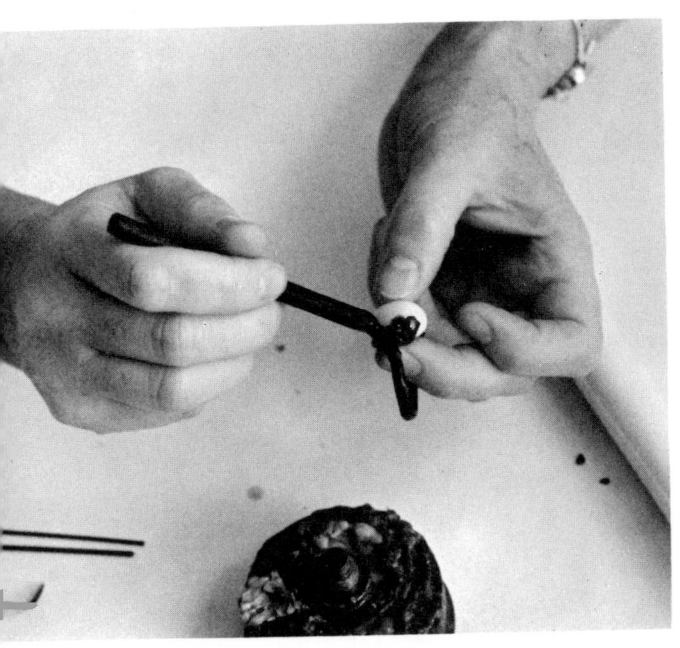

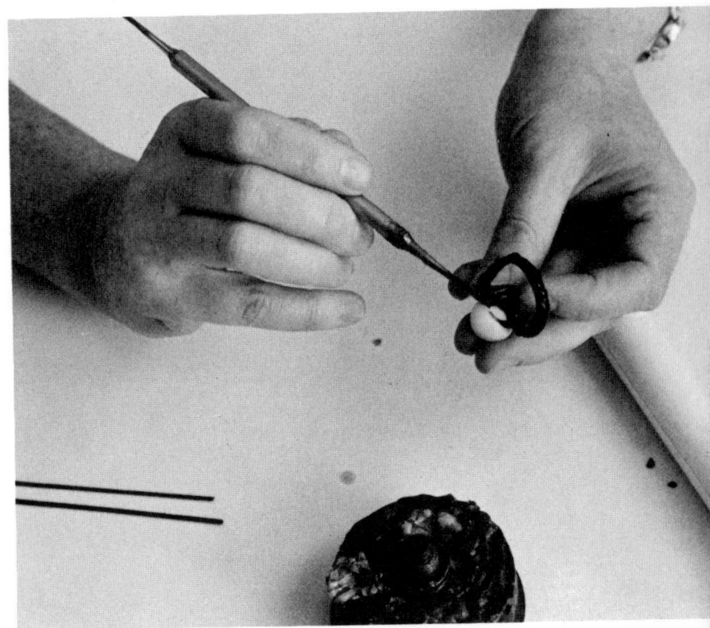

7 and 8. The stone is moistened with glycerine to keep it from sticking, and the base for the stone is begun.

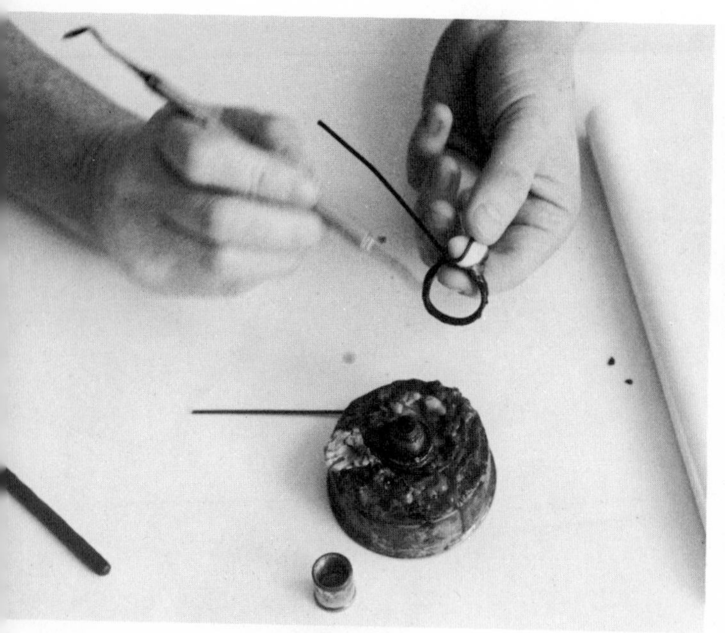

9. Wax wires are used to build the prongs or loops that will hold the stone in place.

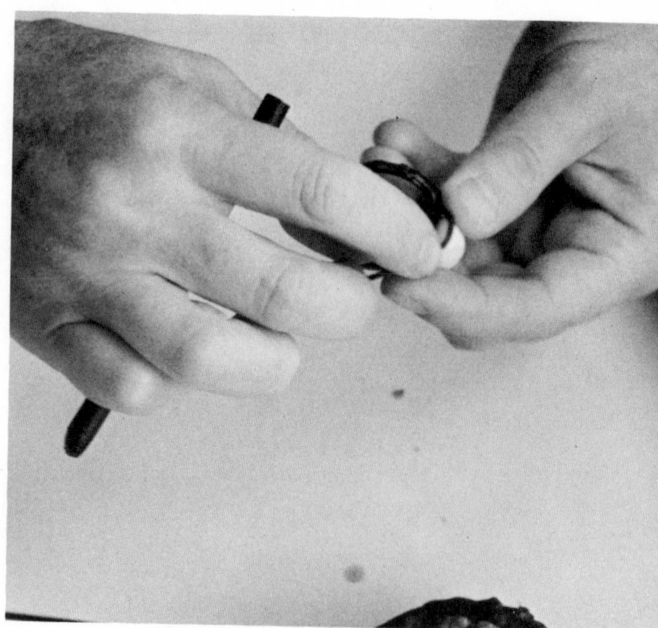

10 and 11. When the base is built, the holding wires are opened slightly to let the stone slip out.

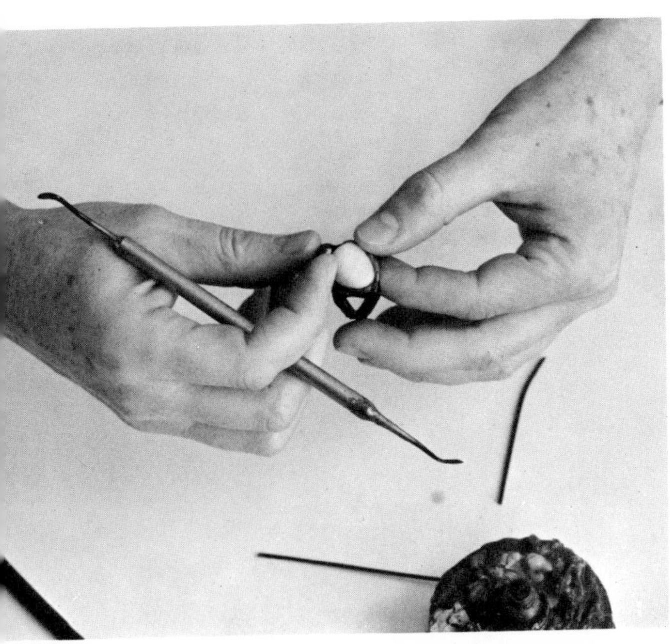

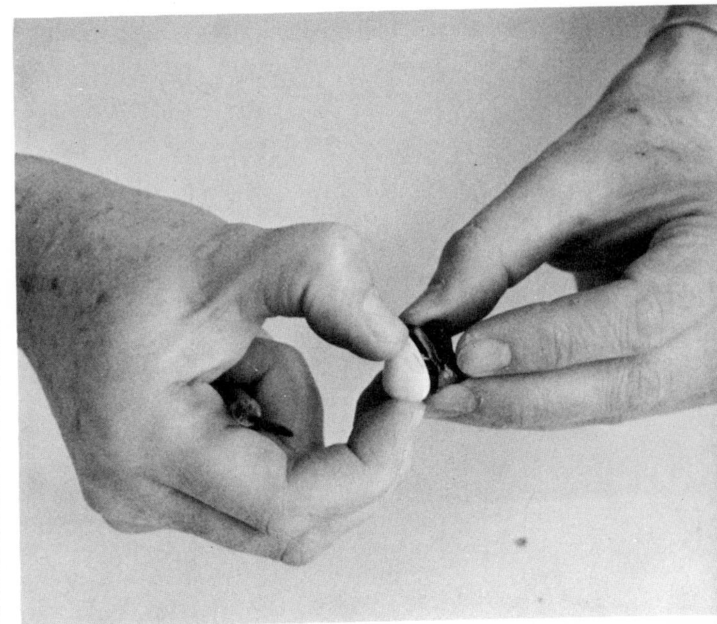

12. The stone is removed, and the ring is ready for casting. It will be cast with the wires that hold the stone in an open position. They will be pushed back only after the piece is cast and ready to set the stone.

Above. Cast gold ring. (Tom Yee.)

Below. Cast gold ring set with a pear-shaped diamond and sapphires. (Tom Yee).

Above. Cast gold ring with black and white opal and diamonds. (Tom Yee.)

Below. Cast gold ring with star sapphire. (Tom Yee.)

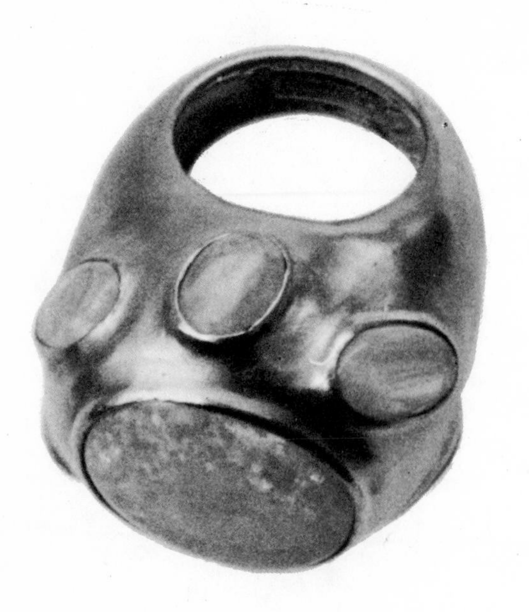

Left. Cast gold domed ring set with opals. (Tom Yee.)

Right. Cast gold ring set with a pearl. (Tom Yee.)

Opposite Page

Cast gold interlocking rings set with a canary diamond and emerald pavé. (Tom Yee.)

1

2

1-6. Wires are joined in a pattern by welding with a hot tool. Wax with plastic in it can be stretched or pulled from one piece of wire to another. Other wires are simply placed in the desired position and then welded in place.

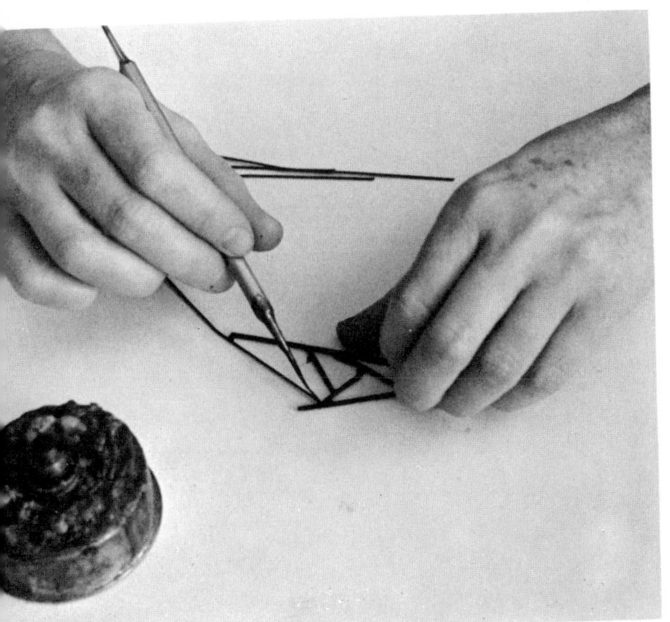

3

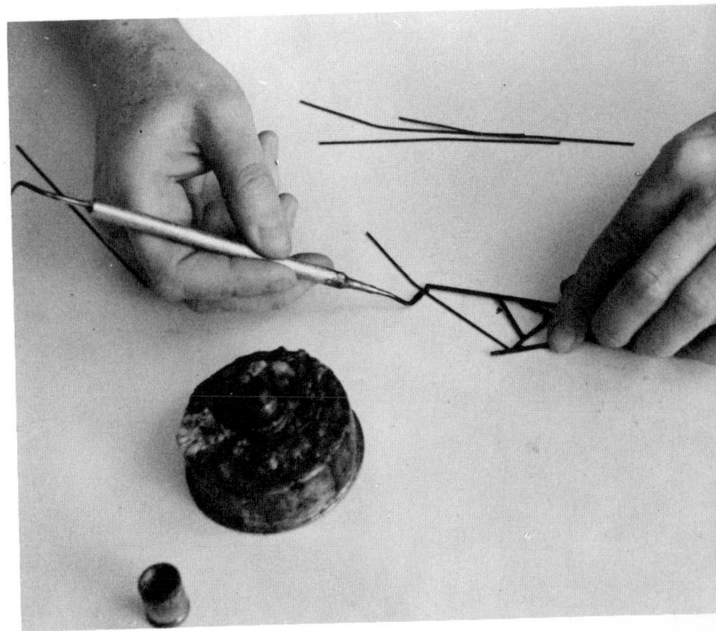

4

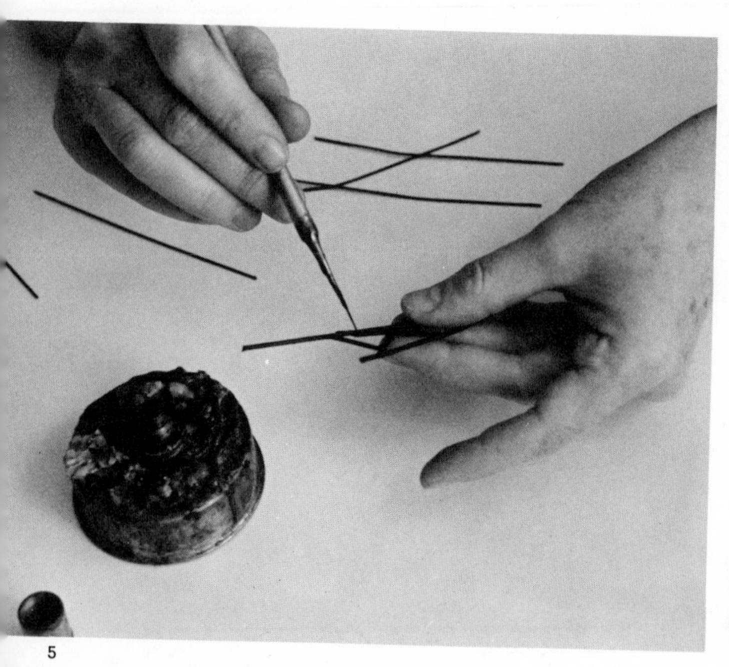

5

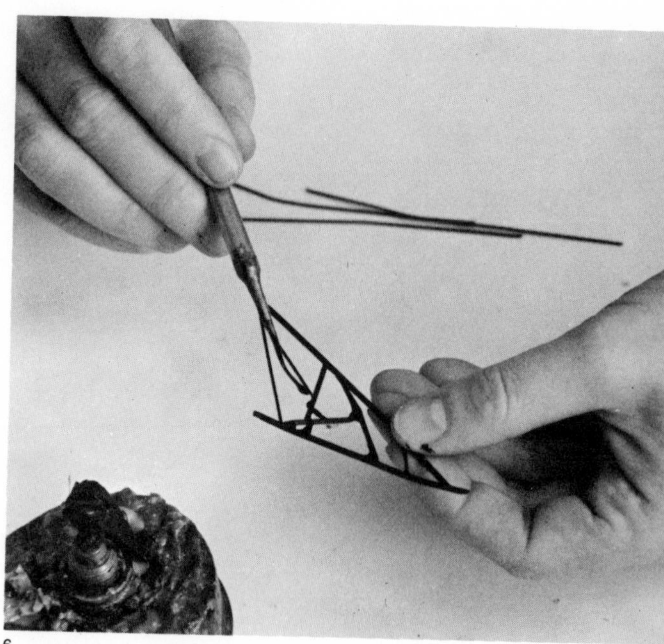

6

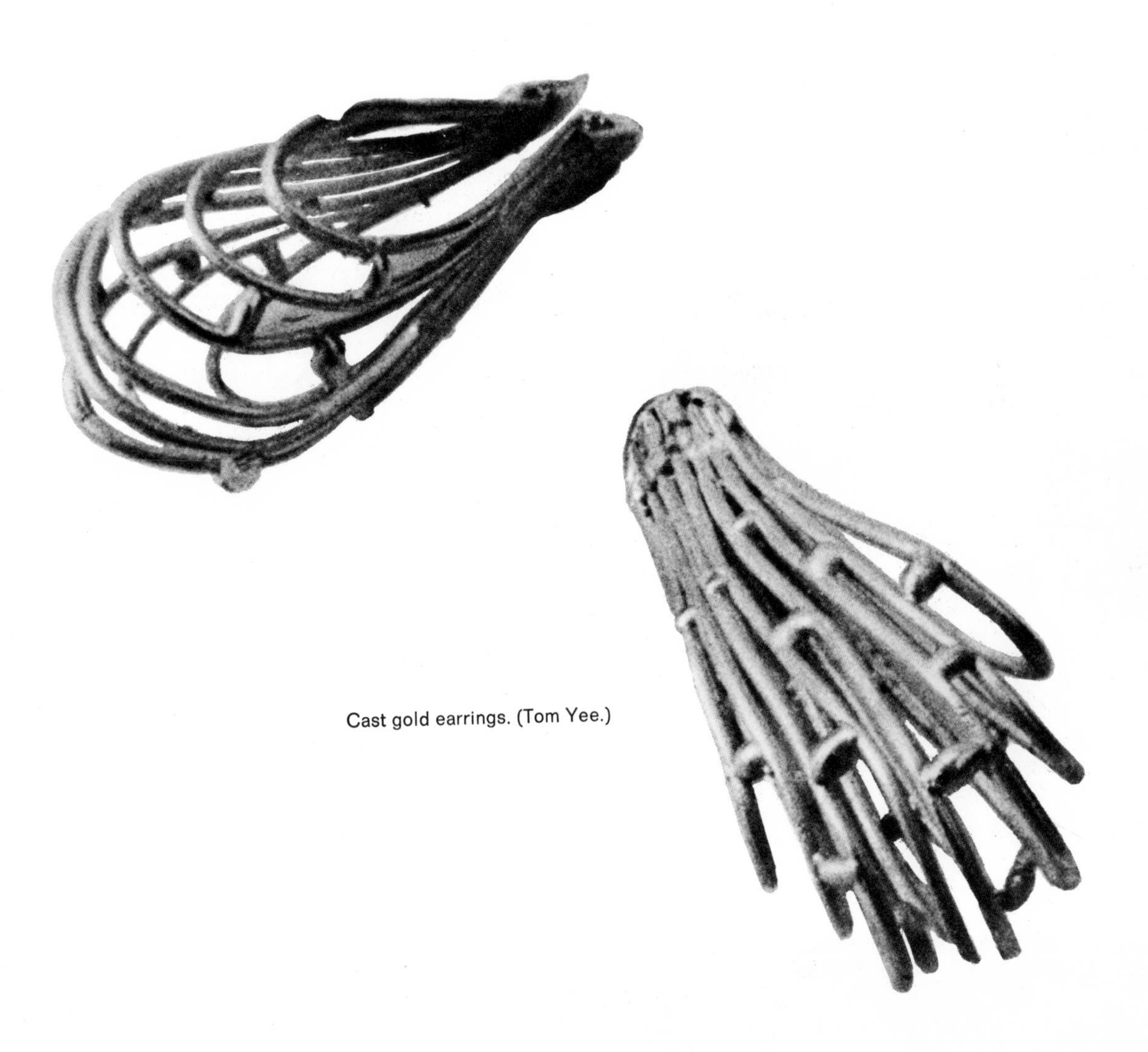

Cast gold earrings. (Tom Yee.)

SCULPTURE

My approach to jewelry and sculpture is the same. Jewelry is done in relation to the human body, sculpture in relation to the space surrounding it. The sculpture shown here is done within the last seven or eight years. Some of the pieces have been done as scale models for larger works. The techniques used are forging, welding, and casting. In some of the sculptures I have used the same design elements as in some of my jewelry, but the relationship to the function of the piece makes the approach to the composition very different.

Opposite Page

Cast gold ring with amethyst. Cast gold brooch set with rutilated quartz. Forged gold earrings. (Tom Yee.)

Memorial cross to John F. Kennedy. Cast in 18-kt. gold with oxidized center, set on a black Japanese pebble. Height: five inches. (Tom Yee.)

Opposite Page

Memorial cross to David Campbell, former Director, American Craftsmen's Council and The Museum of Contemporary Crafts. Cast in gold with small spheres of amethyst, topaz, and moonstone. Height: five inches. (Tom Yee.)

Sculpture of cast silver, set on a black opal, with colored translucent plastic mosaic. Height: six inches. (Tom Yee.)

Opposite Page

Left. Sculpture of forged silver. Height: seventeen inches. (Tom Yee.)

Right. Decanter of fully constructed pewter. Height: ten inches. (Tom Yee.)

Sculpture of forged pewter, crystals, and 24-kt. gold foil. Height: five inches. (Tom Yee.)

Opposite Page

Sculpture of welded iron. Diameter: nine inches. (Tom Yee.)

Right. Rose of chased gold and silver with shell and malachite. Height: four inches. (Tom Yee.)

Below. Flowers of forged gold with garnet and pearl blossoms, set on a beach pebble. Height: two and a half inches. (Tom Yee.)

Daisy of malachite and jelly opal mounted on a green stone. (Tom Yee.)

Three cast gold pill boxes. Reproduced original size. (Tom Yee.)

Bibliography

Choate, Sharr. Creative Castings. New York: Crown Publishing, 1966.

Franke, Lois E. *Handwrought Jewelry*. Bloomington, Illinois: McKnight & McKnight Publishing Co., 1962.

Story, Mickey. *Centrifugal Casting As A Jewelry Process. Scranton,* Pennsylvania: International Text Book Co., 1963.

Wilson, H. *Silverwork and Jewelry. London:* Sir Isaac Pitman & Son, Ltd., 1962.

Suppliers

If not available locally, all equipment, tools, and supplies can be obtained from:

Allcraft Tool and Supply Co., Inc.
22 West 48 Street
New York City
Tel. 212-895-0686

Anchor Tool and Supply Co., Inc.
12 John Street
New York City
Tel. 212-962-2313